Make Sh** Happen

Improve Your Memory

Deborah LeBlanc, CCHt, CAHA

Copyright © 2024 Deborah LeBlanc, CCHt, CAHA

All rights reserved.

The contents of this book may not be reproduced, duplicated, or transmitted without direct written permission from the author.

Under no circumstances will any legal responsibility or blame be held against the publisher for any reparation, damages, or monetary loss due to the information herein, either directly or indirectly.

Legal Notice:

This book is copyright-protected. This is only for personal use. You cannot amend, distribute, sell, use, quote, or paraphrase any part of the content within this book without the consent of the author.

Disclaimer Notice:

Please note the information contained within this document is for educational and entertainment purposes only. Every attempt has been made to provide accurate, up-to-date, reliable, and complete information. No warranties of any kind are expressed or implied. Readers acknowledge that the author is not engaging in the rendering of legal, financial, medical, or professional advice. The content of this book has been derived from various sources. Please consult a licensed professional before attempting any techniques outlined in this book.

By reading this document, the reader agrees that under no circumstances is the author responsible for any losses, direct or indirect, which are incurred as a result of the use of the information contained within this document, including, but not limited to, errors, omissions, or inaccuracies.

Contents

Introduction	1
1. When Sh** Slips Your Mind	4
2. Move Your A**	18
3. Exercise Your Mind	33
4. Unclutter Your Sh**	47
5. Get Some Sleep and Stop Eating Bad Sh**	62
6. Throw Out Sh** Habits	89
7. Use Your Tools and Resources	102
8. Get Your Sh** Together	115
Conclusion	127
About the Author	129

Introduction

Are you tired of forgetting where you left your keys or blanking out on important details? Ever felt the frustration of a foggy memory when you needed it most? Don't worry, as we are here to inject a unique blend of humor and practical wisdom into the art and science of memory enhancement.

This isn't your run-of-the-mill self-help journey. We're not just skimming the surface; we're delving deep into the subtleties of memory improvement. You'll discover the secrets to mental clarity, the power of physical activity, and the wonders of a well-rested mind. It's time to unclutter your thoughts, exercise your brain, and, yes, even throw out a few sh**ty habits that are holding back your memory.

Stay focused as we explore the chapters ahead, each designed to be a steppingstone toward a sharper, more reliable memory. Anticipate hands-on exercises, all rooted in meticulous research and tangible outcomes. Envision this book as an invigorating yet enjoyable terrain where you can cultivate the vast potential residing within your memory.

We'll kick off our journey by confronting the universal experience of forgetfulness: the moments when sh** slips our minds. This chapter is more than an exploration of everyday lapses; it's a deep dive into the importance of mental clarity. We'll explore how a clear mind forms the foundation for positive mental health and consequently an improved memory.

We'll then transition to the vital connection between physical and mental health. You should move your a** not just for the sake of fitness but as a powerful catalyst for mental clarity. Together, we'll explore the ins and outs of an active lifestyle, understanding how it serves not only to invigorate our bodies but also to supercharge our cognitive functions, laying the groundwork for a memory that defies forgetfulness.

Next, we'll step into the mental arena, exploring exercises that will keep your brain agile and ready to tackle memory challenges. We do not limit ourselves to memory tricks; we will lay down a comprehensive guide to the mental exercises to transform your memory from a passive recorder to an active, reliable repository of information.

As we progress, we'll pay particular attention to the importance of uncluttering, which is not just about physical spaces but a mental endeavor with profound implications for mental clarity and wellbeing. We'll explore the numerous benefits of physical, digital, mental, and emotional decluttering, paving the way for a focused, unburdened memory.

We'll then look into how sleep and eating habits, though seemingly unrelated, play a part in improving memory. Quality sleep supports memory consolidation, aiding effective information storage. A well-balanced diet, rich in brain-boosting nutrients, fuels cognitive function for enhanced mental clarity.

Moreover, we'll talk about the importance of habits. From dissecting the procrastination conundrum to building positive habits, this chapter will help you navigate the nuanced landscape of behavioral change. We'll see how tossing out sh**ty habits creates space for positive ones and how this is instrumental in memory improvement.

As we near the end, we'll learn to use the tools and resources at our disposal to enhance memory. From smart devices to calendars, we'll explore how technology can be harnessed to overcome forgetfulness. We can indeed use available resources strategically to reinforce memory in an age of information overload.

Finally, we'll address obstacles and potential challenges. Change your mindset to see them as opportunities to align your thoughts, particularly through meditation and other mindful practices. Your inner stillness will help your mind retain information with greater clarity.

Consider this more than a guide—it's a pledge to reshape your cognitive terrain. Be prepared to gain insights, enjoy moments of laughter, and discover the keys to a memory that goes beyond mere recollection to truly impress. Your journey extends far beyond the last page; it's a launchpad into a life where an enhanced memory becomes a formidable companion in achieving your goals. Are you prepared to embark on this transformative mental odyssey? Let's make sh**t happen and create a memory that lasts a lifetime.

Chapter One

When Sh** Slips Your Mind

Forgetfulness is like that unexpected rain shower: you never see it coming until you're soaked. First, we'll tackle the everyday moments when your keys decide to play hide and seek or names completely disappear from your memory.

We'll then explore the different types of forgetfulness that life throws our way. From transience to blocking, we'll untangle the threads of human memory. We'll also get into the science behind forgetfulness and get into the nitty-gritty of how our brains sometimes play tricks on us. We will naturally conclude that having a clear mind is crucial. It's the flashlight cutting through the forgetfulness fog and the secret to anchoring memories.

Sound Familiar?

At times, our memory can deceive us, and this can happen at times when we least expect it. You leave your house, and two minutes later, while you're already in your car, you suddenly wonder if you locked the door properly. You're telling the story of the incredible movie you saw last week, and as hard as you try, you can't remember the name of the famous actor starring in that movie. In another scenario, you spend two minutes looking for your glasses, even though they are simply sitting on your head. Who has not already experienced at least one situation where their memory seems to want to play hide and seek with them? It's one of the most common human experiences, and we often end up laughing about it because the situation is so ridiculous.

In other cases, forgetting can be less funny. You are about to receive a very important email and you need to log in on a new device that asks for your password. You know the code by heart, but you haven't used it for a few months. You try a few combinations, all incorrect, and your email is blocked. Or you wake up one morning next to the person you love, and they are pouting. You don't understand why, and you spend the day asking them for an explanation. They finally tell you that yesterday was your wedding anniversary. How could you forget something so important? Another situation that can be quite unpleasant is when your boss asks you to prepare something for Thursday morning, and for one reason or another, your brain has decided to completely erase this crucial information from your memory. So you show up at the office on Thursday without knowing that a few minutes later, you will find yourself receiving a warning in your boss's office.

As we have seen, if sometimes our oversights can be anecdotal and a source of amusement, in other cases the consequences can be more serious. In most cases, oversights can be fixed very quickly, but in the rare cases where it can cause problems, it can be a very unpleasant experience.

Types of Forgetfulness

Forgetting is a common part of life, and as we age, it's natural for our memory to undergo some changes. However, distinguishing between normal forgetfulness and potential signs of a more serious issue can be challenging. In this section, we'll explore seven common memory challenges that many individuals encounter, explaining why these lapses occur and when they might indicate a need for closer attention.

- **Transience**

The tendency to forget facts or events over time is a normal aspect of memory. Brain scientists view transience as beneficial as it allows the brain to clear out unused memories, making room for new and more relevant information. Memories that are frequently accessed are less likely to fade away.

- **Absent-Mindedness**

Absent-mindedness occurs when one fails to pay sufficient attention to a task or information. Misplacing items or forgetting to complete tasks are common manifestations of absent-mindedness. The brain may not encode information securely when attention is diverted elsewhere.

- **Blocking**

Temporary memory blocks, where you know the information is there but struggle to retrieve it, become more common with age. This phenomenon might involve recalling a similar memory instead, and research suggests that about half of blocked memories can be retrieved within a minute.

- **Misattribution**

Misattribution involves remembering details inaccurately, such as confusing the time, place, or person related to a memory. With age, misattribution becomes more common, partly due to absorbing fewer details during information acquisition and the aging of existing memories.

- **Suggestibility**

Suggestibility refers to the vulnerability of memory to post-event suggestions. Details learned after an occurrence can become integrated into the memory, creating a distorted recollection. The mechanics of suggestibility in the brain are not fully understood, but it can lead the mind to perceive suggested information as genuine memories.

- **Bias**

A memory is not a flawless snapshot of reality; personal biases influence perceptions during memory encoding. Experiences, beliefs, prior knowledge, and current mood can shape how memories are stored and recalled. While biases affect everyone's memories, the impact of these biases on memory mechanisms remains an understudied area, especially concerning aging.

- **Persistence**

While many people fear forgetting, others grapple with persistent memories of traumatic events, negative emotions, or ongoing fears. This form of memory challenge involves tormenting recollections that individuals wish they could forget but remain vivid. Understanding the mechanisms behind memory persistence is crucial for addressing the impact of traumatic or distressing memories.

To effectively address any issue, the initial crucial step involves gaining a comprehensive understanding of it. Therefore, it becomes imperative to understand the root causes of these memory lapses. What precisely triggers these omissions? Can science enlighten us about the enigma of our faltering memories?

The Science Behind Forgetfulness

Recent insights have shattered conventional views of forgetfulness as a mere hiccup in our cognitive system. Instead, it emerges as a deliberate force, shaped by dedicated neural mechanisms. Imagine your memory like a canvas that keeps getting painted over and erased repeatedly.

Research indicates that a combination of neurotransmitters, proteins, and carbohydrates is involved in creating memories. But we also know that forgetting employs a distinct set of specialized molecular instruments aimed at eliminating information that is no longer pertinent. This marks a paradigm shift, recognizing that our neurons possess a separate toolkit committed to the intentional act of erasing, orchestrating the delicate balance between remembrance and oblivion.

Evolutionary wisdom suggests that forgetting isn't a flaw but a feature, a necessary function ensuring cognitive efficiency. Picture a day in the life of your brain: an unceasing flow of information, some crucial, some inconsequential. Without the ability to forget the trivial details, we'd drown in a sea of irrelevant memories, impeding our capacity to predict, decide, and survive.

In this regard, dopamine emerges as a key player, influencing the brain's ability not just to learn but also to forget temporarily. Indeed, studies on fruit flies suggest that forgetting might be the basal state of the brain,[1] a defense mechanism against information overload. Like a gatekeeper, the brain fights to discard the unnecessary, ensuring that essential memories take center stage when needed.

Forgetfulness, it seems, is also integral to the nightly ritual of sleep. Researchers speculate that the brain's pruning of nonessential memories during sleep contributes to the clarity of mind after a good night's rest.

This delicate process fine-tunes our cognitive landscape, preparing us for the challenges of a new day.

The neuroscience of forgetting also unveils potential links to conditions like autism, PTSD, and Alzheimer's disease. The inability to forget might contribute to behavioral challenges in individuals with autism, emphasizing the importance of the brain's ability to release irrelevant inputs. PTSD, often tied to an excess of synaptic connections, points to the fragile balance between remembering and forgetting.

Mental Clarity Matters

What Is Mental Clarity?

Mental clarity is the state of mind characterized by clear thinking, effective decision-making, and focused concentration on tasks without being overwhelmed or distracted. Achieving and maintaining mental clarity has profound implications for various facets of life, influencing work, relationships, and daily activities.

In a professional context, mental clarity empowers individuals to stay focused on tasks, adeptly manage workloads, and make sound decisions. The result is heightened productivity, improved job performance, and an enhanced sense of accomplishment.

The positive impact extends to interpersonal connections, where mental clarity facilitates more effective communication, active listening, and thoughtful responses, fostering deeper and more meaningful relationships.

Beyond the workplace and relationships, mental clarity plays a pivotal role in managing stress, confronting challenges with composure, and making healthier choices in daily life. This holistic approach to mental clarity contributes to improved physical health, heightened emotional well-being, and an overall enhanced quality of life.

Mental clarity is not an inherent default state; rather, it is a dynamic condition influenced by various factors such as stress and mental fitness. The ups and downs of life can affect cognitive performance, leading to periods where mental clarity may seem elusive. Learning how to enhance mental clarity without succumbing to burnout is crucial for sustaining a productive and engaged lifestyle.

Signs That You Lack Mental Clarity

Identifying a lack of mental clarity is pivotal in addressing underlying issues, as it is a symptom rather than a standalone condition. Stress and anxiety often cast a shadow on cognitive function, leading to mental fatigue and haziness. Recognizing common indicators can shed light on whether you might be experiencing a deficit in mental clarity.

- **Inability to Focus or Concentrate:** If concentrating on a task becomes arduous and demands increased effort, it may signify a lack of mental clarity. In a state of mental well-being, focus is usually effortless. Observing the level of exertion required for concentration provides insights into your current state of mind.

- **Physical or Mental Exhaustion:** Depletion of the mind's energetic resources often manifests in physical and mental exhaustion. Feeling tired and lethargic, especially after minor tasks, can be indicative of low mental clarity. This exhaustion is a signal that behavioral changes may be necessary.

- **Loss of Interest and Motivation:** A diminishing interest in activities that once brought fulfillment is a telling symptom of low mental clarity. When the mind is robust, natural enthusiasm for learning persists. If motivation wanes, it might be a sign that your mind is in need of renewal.

- **Memory Problems:** Memory recall serves as a barometer of mental performance. Strong mental clarity is reflected in efficient memory retention. Conversely, difficulties in recalling memories may point to diminished mental performance. Monitoring the quality of memory recollection offers insights into your mental clarity status.

Recognizing these signs provides a valuable starting point for addressing the root causes and starting the process toward restoring and enhancing mental clarity.

Factors Affecting Mental Clarity

When it comes to mental functioning, mental fog acts as the opposite of clarity, making it challenging to concentrate and maintain focus. Your mind may feel scattered and disconnected. While mental fog doesn't have a singular cause, some factors can increase the likelihood of experiencing this clouded perception. These factors significantly impact your capacity to focus, think clearly, and make decisions. Let's quickly explore each one of them.

- **Lack of Sleep:** Not getting enough sleep affects your mental clarity, making it hard to concentrate and stay focused. The importance of prioritizing adequate sleep cannot be overstated, as it serves as a crucial period for the brain's restoration. During sleep, essential processes such as hormonal balance and neurotransmitter regulation occur, impacting cognitive performance. Prolonged periods without proper sleep result in cognitive impairments, low energy levels, mood fluctuations, and compromised memory function. The Centers for Disease

Control and Prevention (CDC) goes as far as equating staying awake for twenty-four hours with exceeding the legal blood alcohol limit.

- **Stress:** Whether fretting about future uncertainties or dwelling on past stressors, this perpetual state of anxiety can pull you away from the present moment. Chronic stress, known to elevate cortisol levels, adversely impacts circulation, diminishing the flow of oxygen to the brain. As a consequence, mental clarity wanes, exacerbating stress and anxiety levels in a potentially unrelenting cycle.

- **Poor Nutrition:** A holistic approach to nutrition is vital for maintaining optimal physical and mental well-being. Micronutrients and minerals play a crucial role in supporting the intricate functions of the body and mind. When these essential components are lacking, they can have profound effects, affecting not only physical health but also cognitive functions. It is evident that a deficiency in vital nutrients can lead to brain fog and reduced cognitive performance. Furthermore, the quality of nutrition is closely linked to the diversity of one's diet. A lack of variety, coupled with the consumption of a high quantity of processed foods, contributes to poor nutrition.

- **Excessive Technology Use:** In this (arguably) overconnected era, technology poses a significant challenge to staying mentally clear and focused. Distractions abound, from texts and emails to incessant social media notifications, inundating the mind with unnecessary information and diverting attention from the task at hand. The ubiquitous smartphone, a primary source of these distractions, often hinders our ability to be fully present in the moment. Notably, the consequences of phone-related distractions have reached a point where anticipatory anxiety related to notifications has become a recognized phenomenon.

Strategies for Improving Mental Clarity

Maintaining mental clarity has become increasingly crucial for overall well-being and productivity, especially in our fast-paced world. Here are some strategies that can serve as a foundation for improving mental clarity and sharpening your mind.

Stay Active

Regular physical activity is a cornerstone of mental and physical health. Engage in activities that you enjoy, whether it's walking, swimming, or dancing. Physical exercise not only stimulates the circulatory system but also supports mental clarity by promoting the release of neurotransmitters that enhance cognitive function.

Optimize Nutrition

Consider cognitive support supplements and prioritize nutrient-dense foods in your diet, focusing on those rich in omega-3 fatty acids, which are essential for cognitive health. A well-nourished brain is better equipped to tackle daily challenges with clarity and focus.

Try Mindfulness

Incorporate mindfulness practices into your routine and cultivate a heightened sense of awareness. Utilize meditation as a tool for focused attention, allowing your mind to engage with the present moment fully, without being constantly distracted by thoughts and emotions.

Manage Your Time

Prioritize tasks to avoid procrastination, break down larger goals into manageable steps, and plan your days with foresight. This approach not only enhances productivity but also minimizes mental clutter, allowing you to approach each task with a clear and focused mind.

Detox from Technology

Constant digital engagement can overwhelm the mind. Take intentional breaks from devices and set specific limits on technology use. Disconnecting at strategic times, such as during meals or before bedtime, provides your brain with the much-needed respite to recharge and maintain mental clarity.

Sleep Well

Cultivate a consistent sleep schedule, ensuring that you receive the recommended hours of rest each night. Utilize sleep trackers to monitor and enhance your sleep patterns. A well-rested mind is more resilient and better equipped to navigate the challenges of the day.

Reduce Stress

Practice stress management techniques such as deep breathing, gentle stretching exercises, and short walks during breaks. By incorporating them into your routine, you can keep stress at bay and maintain a clear mental state.

Achieve Work-Life Balance

Allocate dedicated time for both work and leisure to achieve a healthy work-life balance. Overcommitting to work can deplete energy levels and lead to burnout, negatively impacting mental clarity. Balancing responsibilities with moments of relaxation and enjoyment contributes to a more focused and resilient mindset.

By incorporating these strategies into your daily life, you can create a robust framework for improving mental clarity. Experiment with these strategies, tailor them to your preferences, and observe the positive impact they can have on your mental well-being.

Benefits of Mental Clarity

Let's explore the great advantages of improving mental clarity and how it can positively impact every facet of your life.

- **Enhanced Decision-Making:** When our minds are clear and focused, decisions naturally align with our best interests and the well-being of those around us. A clouded mind, on the other hand, invites uncertainty. Mental clarity empowers us to analyze complex information, weigh options effectively, and navigate decision-making with precision. By avoiding cognitive biases and decision fatigue, you put yourself in a better position to make objective and rational choices.

- **Stress Mastery:** Managing stress becomes easier with a clear mind. Mental clarity acts as a guiding light in tough times, preventing the onset of overwhelming feelings often triggered by depleted energy and concentration. By keeping our minds in good shape, we handle stress with strength and composure.

- **Efficient Organization:** A clear mind effortlessly handles the chaos of daily responsibilities. It helps with organization, making it easy to prioritize and complete tasks. As the mind becomes a well-ordered workspace, the path to achieving goals becomes easier.

- **Increased Productivity:** Mental clarity allows us to focus on tasks for extended periods, reducing distractions and amplifying productivity. By fostering critical and creative thinking, clarity elevates the quality of our work. The risk of errors diminishes as a clear and focused mind becomes a reliable ally in our pursuit of excellence.

- **Greater Joy in Life:** Having a clear mind helps us enjoy and find meaning in our experiences. It shows you what's important—cherishing time with loved ones and focusing on personal growth. It becomes easier for you to appreciate the beauty of life.

Conclusion

We've talked extensively about forgetfulness, from its various types to the science behind the scenes, and highlighted the absolute necessity of mental clarity. We've laid out the signs so you can call out when your clarity is not at its best. Recognizing it is half the battle. We've also checked out the factors that mess with your mental clarity because without acknowledging them, nothing can be done. Of course, talking about the problem is not enough; we're here to fix them. You've got strategies now—practical tools to amp up mental clarity. It's not rocket science; simple adjustments to your routine can do wonders.

The benefits are worth it. Clear thinking is the backbone of a solid memory. It's a game-changer. So, as you dive back into your life armed with this newfound knowledge, remember this: your memory is yours to own.

---

1. https://time.com/6171190/new-science-of-forgetting/

Chapter Two

Move Your A**

Exercise isn't just about building muscles or squeezing into smaller jeans. Sure, it does wonders for your physical health—trims the waistline, spices up the bedroom, and adds some extra years to the clock—but the real motivation behind staying active goes beyond the surface, deeply effecting our cognitive health—and, by extension, our memory.

People who make exercise a regular part of their lives do it for the feel-good factor. It's not just about looking good; it's about an enormous sense of well-being. They strut through the day with more energy, sleep like logs at night, boast sharper memories, and radiate a relaxed, positive vibe about themselves and their lives.

Regular exercise isn't just a remedy for physical ailments; it's a potent medicine for the mind. It takes on depression and kicks anxiety to the curb. Stress doesn't stand a chance, memory gets an upgrade, and your overall mood? Through the roof.

From understanding our evolutionary roots to discovering practical exercises that come highly recommended, you will see by the end of this chapter why you should leave your couch and start moving.

Evolution Forced Us to Move

Looking at how humans evolved, perpetual movement emerges as a crucial survival strategy ingrained in the very core of our existence. Imagine our ancestors moving across different landscapes, fueled by a relentless need to find food. The transition from rainforests to arid savannahs demanded endurance, with men covering 10-20 kilometers a day and women keeping pace with half that distance. Movement wasn't just a choice; it was a survival imperative.

As the landscape shifted, so did the challenges. Homo erectus, our earliest long-distance walker, showcased a blend of physical endurance and brain growth. Our brains, it seems, evolved not in moments of leisure but in the midst of vigorous physical activity.

The saga continues with the migration of Homo sapiens, spanning continents without the luxuries of maps or advanced tools. The adaptability of our species in the face of diverse environments, from crossing rivers to navigating deserts, speaks volumes about the resilience bred through constant movement.

Now, let's focus on the present. Science is asking interesting questions about the connection between physical activity and thinking abilities. Can getting in better shape boost your cognitive skills?

The Correlation Between Exercise and Brain Health

To grasp the complex connection between exercise and our brains, we need to break down the fundamentals of how our bodies handle food. In a nutshell, the body's process involves breaking down food into glucose, a fundamental energy source. This transformation, achieved through the combined efforts of teeth, acid, and intestines, generates excess electrons known as free radicals. If left unchecked, these electrons can wreak havoc on our cellular structures, posing a potential threat to our overall well-being. Then comes the role of oxygen, a silent but essential player in this biochemical process. Oxygen acts as an efficient sponge, absorbing these excess electrons and transforming them into carbon dioxide through our breath. This process, while seemingly simple, is crucial for maintaining cellular harmony and preventing potential harm caused by free radicals.

How does this relate to the brain? Despite representing a mere 2% of our body weight, it's an energy powerhouse, consuming approximately 20% of our total energy. Maintaining the right balance of glucose and oxygen is crucial for its best performance, providing the energy for the various processes.

In this context, exercise stands out as a modern remedy, bringing a range of benefits that go beyond the physical. The enhanced blood flow throughout the body, attributed to the production of nitric oxide during exercise, improves circulation and not only provides better access to nutrients but also aids in the efficient removal of waste. Exercise particularly optimizes blood flow in the dentate gyrus, a crucial region within the hippocampus associated with memory formation.

At the molecular level, exercise reveals another brain-specific effect. Brain-Derived Neurotrophic Factor (BDNF), a powerful growth factor stimulated by exercise, becomes a significant factor. This protein not only keeps existing neurons healthy and youthful but also encourages neurogenesis, which is the formation of new cells in the brain.

Do You Want to Age Well?

Is there a single key factor that can predict how well you'll age? Researchers have grappled with this question, exploring various factors from genetics to lifestyle. Recently, the scientific community pointed to a powerful influence on aging: whether you lead a sedentary or an active life. In simpler terms, if you're someone who spends a lot of time on the couch, chances are your aging journey might be a bit more challenging. On the flip side, embracing an active lifestyle seems to be the secret sauce for aging well.

Now, what caught researchers by surprise was that those aging well not only had robust physical health but also seemed mentally alert. This prompts a natural follow-up question: how does physical activity relate to mental sharpness?

Test results consistently showed that regular exercise can lead to a remarkable boost in cognitive performance as compared to a sedentary lifestyle. Those who engage in regular physical activity tend to outshine their couch-dwelling counterparts across a spectrum of mental assessments. These assessments cover long-term memory, reasoning, attention, problem-solving, and what's known as fluid intelligence—the ability to think quickly and abstractly to solve new challenges.

Extensive research into aging populations has yielded a somewhat surprising answer to the question of how much exercise is needed for cognitive benefits: not much. Even a simple routine, like regular walks a few times a week, can positively impact the brain.

In laboratory settings, the go-to for optimal cognitive benefits appears to be aerobic exercise: thirty minutes per session two or three times a week. Introducing a strengthening regimen into the mix amplifies these cognitive advantages.

It's important to note that individual responses vary, and before diving into a rigorous exercise routine, consultation with a physician is recommended. Striking the right balance is key, as excessive exercise leading to exhaustion can have detrimental effects on cognition.

In summary, there is one crystal-clear conclusion from the lessons gleaned from our ancestral wanderings to modern science. Everything unequivocally indicates the inherent goodness of exercise for the human brain.

Exercise and Brain Disorders

Exploring the substantial impact of exercise on typical cognitive performance, researchers delved into treating atypical performance, especially concerning diseases like age-related dementia and Alzheimer's disease. The focus extended to affective disorders such as depression, with investigations spanning both prevention and intervention strategies. Drawing upon experiments conducted globally and involving thousands of participants over extended durations, the findings are resoundingly clear.

Engaging in leisure-time physical activity significantly reduces the lifetime risk of general dementia by half. The benefits are even more pronounced with Alzheimer's disease, where regular aerobic exercise reduces the odds of developing the condition by over 60 percent. Notably, a modest commitment to exercise just twice a week can yield substantial benefits. Amplifying this to a daily 20-minute walk not only reduces the risk of stroke—a leading cause of mental disability in the elderly—by 57% but also showcases the transformative potential of regular physical activity.

The inquiry then expanded to examine exercise not merely as a preventive measure but as an intervention for mental disorders like depression and anxiety. Emerging evidence indicates that physical activity significantly influences the course of these diseases, potentially due to its regulation of key neurotransmitters associated with mental health maintenance. While exercise can't replace psychiatric treatment, its profound impact on mood has led many professionals to incorporate physical activity into therapeutic regimens. In some instances, rigorous exercise has even replaced certain medications, showcasing remarkable success in treatment outcomes.

The benefits of exercise extend immediately and persist over the long term for both depression and anxiety. This holds true for individuals of all genders, with the positive effects intensifying with prolonged program duration. Particularly noteworthy is the efficacy of exercise in severe cases and among older individuals.

Exercises for Stress Reduction

In the pursuit of stress reduction, turning to aerobic activities becomes a practical and therapeutic approach. Activities such as brisk walking, jogging, or cycling are more than mere physical exercises; they transform into deliberate rituals designed to alleviate stress. These exercises work dynamically by not only increasing the heart rate but also triggering the release of endorphins—nature's own stress-relievers.

Consider the simplicity of a brisk walk. Each step creates a rhythmic pattern that not only engages the body but also serves as a focused, repetitive motion for the mind. The rhythmic pacing of jogging or the fluidity of cycling further amplifies this effect. As the heart rate escalates, the body responds by releasing endorphins, neurochemicals renowned for their ability to induce feelings of well-being and calm.

What emerges from this deliberate engagement in such activities is a seamless harmony between physical exertion and emotional release. It's not a mystical journey; it's a practical and scientifically-backed approach to managing stress. The beauty lies in the simplicity and accessibility of these exercises, making stress reduction an achievable and integral aspect of your daily routine. So, whether you choose to walk, jog, or cycle, it becomes an effective tool in your self-help arsenal.

Cardio to Elevate Your Mood

Getting into cardio isn't just about working out; it's about feeling good. Whether you're dancing or doing high-intensity intervals, these exercises do more than make you sweat. They boost your mood by improving blood flow and sending more oxygen to your brain.

So your heart's pumping, and it's not just making you healthier; it's also releasing those feel-good chemicals. That's the real magic. You are creating a positive vibe that lasts beyond your workout. So, whether you're hitting the dance floor or pushing through intervals, cardio becomes your key to feeling lively and happy, making every session an investment in your overall well-being.

Strength Training for Cognitive Resilience

Engaging in strength training extends beyond visible gains in muscle mass; it significantly contributes to mental well-being. As you lift weights or perform resistance exercises, the physiological response goes beyond the physical aspect to impact your cognitive and emotional state. Scientifically, strength training prompts the release of neurotransmitters like endorphins, which act as natural mood enhancers, reducing feelings of stress and anxiety. The discipline required for consistent strength training fosters a sense of accomplishment and empowerment, contributing to improved self-esteem and mental resilience.

Furthermore, the focus and concentration demanded during strength-training sessions create a form of mindfulness, diverting attention from daily stressors. The progressive nature of strength training, as individuals witness their own physical advancements, instills a positive mindset and a belief in one's capabilities that transcends the gym setting. Additionally, the hormonal balance achieved through strength training, including the reduction of cortisol, the stress hormone, further consolidates its positive impact on mental health.

Tailor Your Routine

Customizing your exercise routine is key to its effectiveness. Incorporating a mix of aerobic, strength, and flexibility exercises creates a well-rounded regimen. Each component plays a distinct role in enhancing your mental health. Aerobic exercises elevate your heart rate, promoting overall cardiovascular health and mental clarity. Strength training fosters physical resilience, contributing to a sense of accomplishment and mental fortitude. Flexibility exercises support joint health and agility, adding a crucial element to your overall well-being. The synergy of these diverse exercises brings tangible benefits each brings to the table.

Enjoy It

Find pleasure in your exercise routine. Opt for activities that align with your unique preferences, be it the tranquility of hiking, the delight of dancing, or the discipline of martial arts. The key is to choose workouts that resonate with your individuality, transforming them into enjoyable and enduring elements of your routine. This way, exercise becomes more than a task—it becomes a source of satisfaction and fulfillment, ensuring that staying active is not just a goal but a pleasurable part of your lifestyle.

Adapt as Needed

Maintain a keen awareness of your body and mind throughout your fitness journey. Be attuned to the subtle signals your body sends during and after each workout, and create space for adjustments. This conscientious approach ensures that every exercise session becomes a personalized response to your present mental and physical state. By staying receptive to your body's cues, flexibility becomes a vital part of your exercise routine.

Reflect on how your workouts impact your mood, energy levels, and overall well-being. It's an ongoing dialogue between you and your body where adjustments are made organically, ensuring that your fitness journey remains fluid and tailored to your evolving needs. It's a deliberate and intelligent strategy that allows your fitness routine to grow and evolve alongside you.

Micro-Exercises for Busy Lifestyles

Life can be a chaotic journey, and carving out space for a comprehensive workout may seem like an unattainable feat. This is where micro-exercises step in as your allies. Envision swift, energetic movements meticulously crafted for individuals with demanding lifestyles—individuals just like yourself. These compact, impactful bursts of activity effortlessly integrate into your daily routine: a brisk stretch here, a brief cardio surge there. Even the most hectic schedules can accommodate a sprinkle of self-care.

Incorporating Movement into Daily Tasks

Ever thought about weaving movement into your daily hustle? It's a game-changer. Swap that elevator ride for a stair climb, add desk stretches into your workday, or sneak in quick exercises during coffee breaks. You don't need to disrupt your schedule; it's about making movement a natural sidekick to your daily tasks. This will make you feel energized without a major overhaul. That's the beauty of incorporating movement effortlessly.

Consult a Professional

When uncertainties arise, don't hesitate to turn to the expertise of fitness professionals or healthcare providers for valuable guidance. Seeking advice from these professionals adds a practical layer to your fitness journey. They can offer personalized insights tailored to your individual needs, helping you align your exercise routine with specific mental health goals. These professionals possess the knowledge to consider your physical condition and potential limitations, ensuring that your approach to fitness is not only effective but also safe. Their practical recommendations may include suitable exercises, modifications, or even alternative strategies to address any concerns or challenges you might encounter. Embracing the guidance of professionals not only enhances the practicality of your fitness endeavors but also instills confidence in the choices you make.

Mindful Movement

Mindful movement, including practices such as yoga, Tai Chi, and similar disciplines, unfolds a transformative journey toward holistic well-being. In the daily hustle, where stress and demands usually take over, these mindful exercises become useful tools to boost physical health and clear your mind.

Yoga, with its roots in ancient wisdom, is not a mere physical exercise. Beyond the dynamic postures and flexibility it builds, yoga integrates breath control and meditation, creating a unique space for mental rejuvenation. The deliberate focus on the breath, synchronized with movement, instills a sense of mindfulness, a heightened awareness of the present moment. With its diverse styles and approaches, yoga allows individuals to explore and discover what resonates with them. Whether it's the flowing sequences of Vinyasa or the precise alignment of Iyengar, each style offers a unique avenue for self-discovery

Tai Chi, characterized by slow, flowing movements, also emerges as a profound contributor to mental tranquility. This martial art, rooted in Chinese philosophy, emphasizes balance, flexibility, and a mindful state. The deliberate pace of Tai Chi allows practitioners to synchronize their movements with deep-breathing techniques, promoting not just physical harmony but also a calm and centered mental state. It becomes like a moving meditation.

These practices become a form of mental resilience, offering a shield against the stressors of daily life. Left unchecked, stress can manifest as mental fog and hinder cognitive function. Yoga and Tai Chi act as antidotes, providing a structured approach to stress reduction. The intentional and meditative nature of these practices activates the body's relaxation response, countering the detrimental effects of chronic stress on mental clarity.

Mindful movement becomes a bridge between physical and mental health. It's not merely about executing postures or following choreographed sequences; it's about creating an internal shift to a precious harmony between body and mind. The benefits ripple through various facets of life, from improved sleep quality to increased emotional resilience.

Technology and Fitness

We live in a digital era, and there is great opportunity to integrate technology with your path to better fitness. Imagine this: your very own team of fitness apps, wearables, and virtual workout platforms working harmoniously to reshape how you engage with physical activity. These technological comrades aren't just tools; they're your dedicated allies, providing instantaneous feedback on your progress, delivering workout plans meticulously tailored to your needs, and fostering a community ambiance that makes your fitness venture particularly exciting. Bid farewell to monotonous routines as you step into the future of fitness, where a world of personalized, motivating experiences awaits at the tap of your fingertips.

Post-Exercise Recovery

What comes after your workout grind? Your commitment doesn't stop there. Your muscles are longing for some extra care, and that's where post-exercise recovery kicks in. Hydration, nutrition, and practices like stretching or foam rolling become your go-to resources. It's not merely about easing sore muscles; it's about taking care of your body after the sweat session, making sure you not only tackle your workout but also come out feeling refreshed and geared up for what's next.

Community Fitness Events

Think of fitness beyond a solo expedition; visualize it as a shared celebration within a community. Envision yourself partaking in charity runs, joining group fitness classes, or engaging in local sports leagues, all while surrounded by individuals who share your passion. You will not only work up a sweat; you will build connections, celebrate collective successes, and enjoy a shared path toward well-being. Your participation isn't only about your individual success; it plays a role in motivating others and contributing to shared accomplishments in your community.

Making Exercise a Habit

Trying to achieve mental clarity through regular exercise can be challenging, and common obstacles may discourage even the most motivated individuals. Understanding and overcoming these obstacles is crucial for transforming physical activity into a sustainable habit.

- **Barrier 1: Time Constraints:** Many individuals cite lack of time as a primary impediment to regular exercise. Balancing work, family, and personal commitments can be challenging. However, reframing priorities and recognizing the profound impact of exercise on mental well-being can help carve out dedicated time. Even short, focused sessions can yield significant benefits.

- **Strategy: Prioritize and Schedule:** Acknowledging the importance of mental health, carve out specific time slots for exercise in your daily or weekly schedule. Treat these appointments with the same seriousness as work meetings or other commitments. By prioritizing exercise, you reinforce its significance in your routine.

- **Barrier 2: Lack of Motivation:** Maintaining consistent motivation can be elusive. The initial enthusiasm may wane, making it challenging to stick to an exercise regimen. However, understanding the intrinsic link between physical activity and mental clarity provides a compelling reason to persist.

- **Strategy 2: Set Realistic Goals:** Establish achievable and realistic fitness goals. Whether it's committing to a certain number of weekly workouts or gradually increasing exercise intensity, setting manageable objectives keeps motivation alive. Celebrate small victories to reinforce a positive association with exercise.

- **Barrier 3: Boredom and Monotony:** Repetitive exercise routines can become monotonous, leading to boredom and eventual disinterest. Combating this requires injecting variety and enjoyment into your workouts.

- **Strategy 3: Diversify Activities**: Experiment with various forms of exercise to keep things interesting. From outdoor activities like hiking or cycling to group classes or team sports, finding enjoyment in movement makes exercise a pleasure rather than a chore.

- **Barrier 4: Physical Discomfort or Health Concerns:** For some, physical discomfort or health issues may pose genuine barriers to exercise. Addressing these concerns with appropriate modifications and seeking professional advice is essential for a safe and sustainable approach.

- **Strategy 4: Consultation and Adaptation:** Consult with healthcare professionals or fitness experts to tailor your exercise routine to your specific needs and health conditions. Whether it involves modifying certain movements or exploring low-impact alternatives, personalized adjustments ensure safety and comfort.

Consistency is key, and it's essential to recognize that overcoming these barriers requires a combination of self-awareness, adaptability, and a commitment to long-term well-being. By proactively addressing challenges and incorporating these strategies, individuals can transform exercise from a sporadic activity into an ingrained, life-enriching habit conducive to mental clarity.

Conclusion

We've explored why moving is in our DNA, how it's a brain booster, and why it's the key to aging like a champ. We've tackled brain disorders, personalized your exercise plan, and explored the power of mindful movement.

But here's the real deal: it's not just about physical perks. It's about making exercise an integral part of your life, not some daunting task. It's not a one-size-fits-all thing; it's about what works for you.

So, as we close this chapter, keep it simple. Your body craves movement. Whether you're powerlifting or taking a leisurely stroll, the important thing is you're moving.

Picture a future where movement isn't a chore but a joy. Your body, mind, and spirit deserve it.

Chapter Three

Exercise Your Mind

Just as we prioritize physical exercise to maintain our bodily health, the importance of exercising our minds becomes increasingly evident, particularly as we age. The adage "use it or lose it" applies to mental faculties as well as physical fitness. Just as lifting weights strengthens our muscles, engaging in activities that fortify our mental "muscles" proves essential for improving memory, attention, brain speed, people skills, intelligence, and even navigation skills.

Variety stands as the key principle in this endeavor. Like changing our workout routines to continually challenge our bodies, exercising our minds requires introducing variety into our mental activities. If a mental task becomes too easy and second nature, it signifies an opportunity to enhance brainpower by increasing the difficulty level. For instance, mastering a crossword puzzle in record time prompts us to seek more challenging variations, ensuring that our brains remain actively engaged and responsive.

This chapter explores brain exercises and their transformative impact on cognitive well-being. Regardless of age, individuals can reap benefits by incorporating a few minutes of daily brain exercises into their routines. Scientific studies emphasize the efficacy of consistent, shorter sessions over sporadic, longer ones in optimizing cognitive health. Just as we invest time in a balanced diet and regular physical activity for overall well-being, dedicating a few minutes each day to exercising our minds proves equally indispensable.

The following sections explore practical ways to reach optimal mental fitness, offering insights and exercises that go beyond the conventional narratives surrounding brain training.

The Importance of Neuroplasticity

What Is Neuroplasticity?

Neuroplasticity is a foundational concept that allows us to understand the brain's remarkable adaptability. It reveals the extraordinary nature of our neural architecture. The brain, far from being static, continuously undergoes structural and functional changes throughout our lives. This adaptive capacity enables it to reorganize in response to various stimuli, experiences, and environmental factors. At its core, neuroplasticity challenges the long-held notion that the brain's neural pathways are fixed and unalterable. Instead, it emphasizes the dynamic and malleable nature of the brain's intricate network of neurons.

Whether it's learning a new skill, acquiring knowledge, or adapting to life's challenges, the brain remains in a constant state of flux. This adaptability is not confined to specific developmental stages but is an ongoing process. Recognizing the dynamic nature of neuroplasticity underscores the potential for continuous growth and development, providing a scientific foundation for the concept that our brains can evolve, adapt, and thrive constantly. This insight is pivotal in understanding how intentional efforts to stimulate the brain through various activities can harness neuroplasticity for personal growth and cognitive enhancement.

Types of Neuroplasticity

Neuroplasticity appears in different ways, and two significant aspects define the brain's adaptability: structural and functional plasticity.

Structural plasticity involves physically reorganizing the brain's architecture. This includes creating new connections between synapses and eliminating unnecessary ones through synaptic pruning. This ongoing rewiring helps the brain fine-tune its neural circuitry, making it more efficient and adaptable to changing demands.

On the other side, *functional* plasticity refers to the brain's knack for shifting functions from damaged to undamaged areas. When faced with injury or stress, the brain can dynamically reroute neural pathways, displaying remarkable resilience. This adaptive process contributes to recovery after trauma, stroke, or other neurological challenges.

These processes create opportunities for therapeutic interventions, offering hope for those undergoing neurological rehabilitation. They clearly demonstrate the brain's ability to regenerate and optimize.

Factors Influencing Neuroplasticity

Neuroplasticity is significantly influenced by various factors that dictate the pace and extent of its dynamic changes. First of all, there is the frequency of new experiences. Continuous exposure to fresh stimuli enhances the brain's flexibility, favoring an environment conducive to adaptive changes.

The richness of the environment represents another crucial factor. A stimulating environment characterized by a variety of experiences and sensory inputs is instrumental in promoting neuroplasticity. The brain thrives in diverse settings where it is consistently exposed to different challenges and stimuli. This enriching environment contributes to the creation of a neural landscape that is agile, responsive, and poised for adaptation.

Moreover, neuroplasticity is closely linked to neurochemical factors. The role of neurotransmitters and growth factors cannot be overstated in either facilitating or inhibiting plastic changes within the brain. These chemical messengers play a crucial role in regulating the strength and efficacy of neural connections.

Implications of Neuroplasticity

Learning and Memory

Neuroplasticity plays a pivotal role in the processes of learning and memory formation within the human brain. This phenomenon underscores the brain's remarkable ability to adapt and reorganize itself based on experiences and stimuli. When we engage in learning activities, the brain responds by creating and reinforcing neural connections, a process critical to the retention of information. These connections, known as synapses, serve as the building blocks for memory, allowing the brain to encode, store, and retrieve information effectively.

This dynamic process is particularly pronounced during periods of acquiring new skills or knowledge. As we expose ourselves to novel information or engage in challenging tasks, the brain's neural circuits undergo changes to accommodate the incoming data.

Neurotransmitters, the chemical messengers facilitating communication between neurons, play a crucial role in this process. Understanding the interaction between neural pathways, synapse formation, and neurotransmitter activity sheds light on the profound connection between neuroplasticity and the cognitive processes fundamental to our ability to learn, adapt, and remember throughout our lives. Harnessing this knowledge empowers individuals to optimize their learning potential and cognitive capabilities through intentional and targeted mental activities.

Overcoming Limiting Beliefs

Neuroplasticity empowers individuals to confront and conquer limiting beliefs. The brain's ability to rewire itself means that negative thought patterns and self-doubt can be consciously challenged and changed. By intentionally reshaping one's mindset, individuals can break free from self-imposed limitations, facilitating personal growth, and unlocking their full potential.

Neurofeedback and Brain Training

Technologies like neurofeedback capitalize on neuroplasticity principles. Real-time information about brain activity is provided, allowing individuals to observe and understand their mental processes. Utilizing this feedback, brain training programs can be designed to enhance specific functions, such as concentration or emotional regulation. By engaging with targeted brain exercises, individuals leverage neuroplasticity to achieve desired outcomes.

Recovery and Rehabilitation

Neuroplasticity emerges as a crucial mechanism that can be harnessed to facilitate the restoration of lost functions following brain injuries or strokes. By engaging in specific activities tailored to the individual's needs, these interventions encourage the brain to reroute functions to undamaged areas. This process involves creating new neural connections and adapting existing pathways to compensate for areas that may have been affected by injury or trauma.

Rehabilitation, in this context, becomes a dynamic and personalized endeavor. The intentional design of exercises and therapies aligns with the principles of neuroplasticity and offers a structured approach to rebuilding cognitive and motor functions. As individuals undergo targeted interventions, they actively participate in the rewiring of their neural circuitry. This approach also instills hope and resilience in individuals undergoing rehabilitation, as they work towards reclaiming lost abilities.

Mental Health

Neuroplasticity plays a practical role in mental health by illustrating the brain's ability to change and adapt. For instance, individuals dealing with anxiety can benefit from mindfulness practices that reshape neural pathways associated with stress response. Therapies like Cognitive Behavioral Therapy (CBT) actively utilize neuroplasticity to help individuals reframe negative thought patterns and habitual harmful emotions. Additionally, establishing consistent routines, such as regular exercise and quality sleep, supports neuroplasticity and contributes to improved mood and overall mental health. Engaging in positive habits and therapeutic interventions can create tangible changes in the brain, and it provides a concrete pathway for individuals struggling with mental health issues.

How to Exercise Your Brain

- **Read a Variety of Books:** Books are filled with interesting characters, infinite information, and facts. Challenge your brain by reading a variety of topics, from historical fiction to contemporary classics to romance. Your brain will get a workout imagining different time periods, cultures, and people while learning new things and building vocabulary. Plus, you'll be developing interesting stories to share with others.

- **Use All Your Senses:** Activities that simultaneously engage your senses, like cooking or gardening, provide rich experiences that not only tantalize the senses but actively contribute to the strengthening of cognitive functions. The immersive experience of smelling, touching, tasting, seeing, and hearing all at once is likened to a comprehensive workout for both your senses and your brain. Whether it's the vibrant atmosphere of a food festival or the culinary exploration of a new restaurant, the emphasis is on holistic sensory engagement.

- **Meditate:** If there is a practice that can change your life, it is meditation. At the beginning of your journey, dedicate just five minutes each day to meditation to reap a myriad of benefits. Beyond instilling calmness and reducing stress, this practice has the potential to enhance both memory and cognitive processing abilities by cultivating a serene mental state. Research supports the profound impacts of meditation, revealing associations with increased neuroplasticity, reduced brain aging, and overall improvements in cognitive abilities. Practicing meditation involves creating a serene space, free from disturbances, where you can sit or lie down comfortably. Close your eyes gently or maintain a soft gaze as you turn your attention to your breath, observing its natural rhythm. You can also focus on a specific point, sound, or mantra, to gently guide your mind back if it wanders. Start with brief sessions, gradually extend the duration, and be patient with yourself. Explore various meditation techniques, such as mindfulness or loving-kindness, to find what resonates with you. You can also consider utilizing guided meditation resources to provide structure and support, allowing your meditation practice to naturally evolve and strengthen.

- **Learn a New Skill:** Unlocking the potential of your brain is an ageless process, and learning a new skill stands out as a powerful way to achieve it. Regardless of your age, engaging in the process of acquiring a fresh skill not only introduces excitement into your life but also strengthens the intricate web of connections within your brain. When you challenge yourself, various brain areas come into play — memory, motor skills, and associative thinking all collaborate.

A study[1] investigating the impact of learning on memory found that older adults who took on the challenge of acquiring new skills experienced notable improvements compared to those engaging in less mentally demanding activities. Notably, the memory enhancements persisted even a year later, showcasing the enduring benefits of acquiring new knowledge. This reinforces the idea that committing to learning a new skill is a valuable investment in cognitive vitality. So, whether it's immersing yourself in the art of photography or exploring the world of coding, the pursuit of new skills emerges as a compelling and rewarding journey that contributes not only to personal development but also to the vitality of your mind.

- **Teach a New Skill:** Boost your learning by teaching a new skill to someone else. After picking up a skill, practice it, and then explain the steps to another person. For instance, if you learn how to bake a cake or ride a bike, share those steps with a friend. This not only deepens your understanding of the skill but also gives you a chance to fix any mistakes. It's a collaborative way to learn and improve together. The journey becomes even more enriching when you share it with others, and it solidifies your newfound knowledge and reinforces the brain's plasticity.

- **Draw a Map from Memory:** Boost your brainpower by trying a new way to explore your usual surroundings. Instead of following the usual routes you know by heart, challenge yourself by sketching a map of your town or neighborhood from memory. Take on the challenge without using any reference materials, and try to include main streets, side streets, and main tourist attractions.

After completing your memory map, compare it with an actual map of the area. Identify any inaccuracies or omissions. If this exercise proves too easy, elevate the difficulty by drawing a less familiar area from memory, such as a comprehensive map of the United States or Europe, and challenge yourself to label every state or country.

Similar cognitive challenges were examined in a study involving London taxi drivers, a group required to memorize the city map. The results indicated that drivers who successfully committed the map to memory experienced enduring structural changes in their brains accompanied by enhanced cognitive function. This underscores the profound impact of cognitive exercises on brain structure and cognitive capabilities.

- **Use Your Non-Dominant Hand:** Unlock the potential of your mind by delving into an unconventional exercise recommended by neurobiologist Lawrence Katz. He suggests harnessing the power of your non-dominant hand to fortify your cognitive abilities. The rationale behind this recommendation lies in the inherent challenge of using your opposite hand, making it a potent strategy to elevate brain activity.

Embrace this mental workout by incorporating the use of your non-dominant hand into everyday activities. Consider switching hands while dining or attempting to jot down notes. Although mastering this skill may prove initially difficult, the challenge itself becomes the focal point, igniting heightened brain engagement. Unconventional methods stimulate your mind and fortify its neural connections.

- **Socialize:** Uncover the profound impact of social engagement on cognitive health. Studies show a significant link between social activity and a reduced risk of dementia and Alzheimer's disease. Explore diverse social avenues such as volunteering, social sports, club participation, and local running groups, and cherish meaningful connections with friends and family. The joy derived from socializing transcends mere leisure; it stands as a potent stimulant for the brain.

- **Build Your Vocabulary:** Expanding your vocabulary not only makes you sound brilliant and articulate but also provides a stimulating workout for your brain. Engaging in vocabulary tasks activates various regions of the brain, particularly those crucial for visual and auditory processing, as supported by research.

To turn this into a cognitive game, incorporate a simple activity into your routine. Keep a notebook handy while reading or watching TV, jot down an unfamiliar word, and discover its definition. Challenge yourself to incorporate this new word into your vocabulary by using it at least five times the next day.

Listen to or Play Music: As evidenced by research findings, engaging with music has many benefits for cognitive function and creativity.

Playing a musical instrument emerges as a powerful tool for cognitive development and offers advantages for both the young and aging brain. The act of playing instruments not only supports cognitive growth in youth but also acts as a protective factor against cognitive decline in later years.

Learning a musical instrument or joining a choir comes with the assurance that age is no hindrance to acquiring new skills. Contrary to the belief that learning diminishes with age, findings emphasize that it's never too late to start playing instruments like the piano, guitar, or drums.

- **Learn a New Language:**. Numerous research studies highlight the positive impact of bilingualism on cognitive functions. Proficiency in more than one language is linked to enhanced memory, improved visual-spatial skills, and heightened creativity. Beyond these benefits, fluency in more than one language facilitates smoother task-switching and may delay the onset of age-related mental decline.

The encouraging aspect is the timeless nature of language learning rewards. Research indicates that individuals can enhance memory and other mental functions by learning a new language at any stage of life. The cognitive benefits extend to brain stimulation through the auditory processes involved in language acquisition. Additionally, bilingualism demonstrates a potential safeguard, with research indicating a lower risk of developing Alzheimer's disease and other forms of dementia in individuals fluent in multiple languages.

- **Use Visualization:** Visualization is a technique to create mental images that represent information. These mental images may manifest in various forms from still pictures to animated scenes. Insights from a 2018 review[2] highlight the efficacy of visualization in helping individuals structure information and make well-informed decisions. The practical application of visualization extends to everyday scenarios. Here's an example: picturing yourself successfully completing a particular task before starting it can boost your confidence and performance. The essence lies in crafting these mental scenes with vivid clarity and details for optimal effectiveness.

- **Challenge Your Memory:** Create a list, be it grocery items or tasks to accomplish, and commit it to memory. Revisit the list an hour later and test your recall. Try to make the list as challenging as possible for optimal mental stimulation. Studies suggest that the act of writing and organizing lists significantly improved word list recall in older adults.

- **Do Math Calculations in Your Head:** Tackle problems without relying on external aids like pencil, paper, or computer. It's been indicated that solving math problems positively impacts cognition.

- **Cook:** Cooking engages multiple senses—smell, touch, sight, and taste—activating different parts of the brain. Additionally, it hones cognitive skills such as meal planning, problem-solving, creating grocery lists, multitasking, and organizing.

- **Sharpen Your Hand/Eye Coordination:**. Engage in a new hobby like racquet sports, knitting, drawing, painting, or playing video games. These pursuits not only keep your hand/eye coordination sharp but also contribute to the overall enhancement of cognitive abilities.

- **Engage in a New Hobby:** Explore a new hobby to provide mental stimulation and challenge your brain in novel ways. Opt for hobbies that demand coordination and dexterity and activate crucial motor skills. Engage in activities like knitting, painting, or dancing to not only enjoy a fulfilling pastime but also to stimulate various cognitive functions.

- **Play Games:** Engaging in specific brain exercises improves memory, concentration, and focus. These games rely on logic, math, and visuospatial skills, and challenge your brain.

For example, think of the joy of assembling a jigsaw puzzle, whether it's a 1,000-piece depiction of the Taj Mahal or a 200-piece image of Spiderman. Research indicates that this activity recruits various cognitive abilities, serving as a protective factor for visuospatial cognitive aging.

Rediscover timeless board games like chess or checkers, which have demonstrated positive impact on memory, executive functioning, and information-processing speed.

Video games are not just for kids, particularly those involving action and strategy genres. They may lead to improvements in attention, problem-solving, and cognitive flexibility.

Revisit traditional card games like solitaire, bridge, gin rummy, poker, or hearts. A 2015 study[3] suggests that engaging in card games can contribute to larger brain volume and improved cognitive health markers, especially in individuals at risk of Alzheimer's disease. Embrace the simplicity of a card game, and witness not only the enjoyment it brings but also its potential to enhance memory and thinking skills.

This diverse array of activities showcases the different and enjoyable ways you can cultivate a sharp and resilient mind. As an adult, if you're looking for a compelling reason to spend some time playing games, now you have one.

Conclusion

In conclusion, prioritizing your brain health emerges as a cornerstone for enhancing key cognitive functions such as concentration, focus, memory, and mental agility, irrespective of age. The incorporation of brain exercises into your daily routine offers a dynamic opportunity to not only challenge your mind but to sharpen cognitive skills while following a path of continuous learning and enrichment. Ranging from everyday tasks that actively engage the brain to targeted workouts designed to boost memory, cognition, or creativity, these exercises contribute to improved brain function and enhanced connectivity among different brain areas, potentially safeguarding against age-related degeneration.

Individuals have diverse preferences, so it is advisable to explore a variety of brain-training activities initially and then adhere to those that provide the utmost enjoyment or reward. The compelling evidence supporting the importance of living a brain-healthy lifestyle, combined with the joy these activities bring, shows why it's crucial to take proactive steps to protect our brain's long-term health and vitality.

---

1. https://journals.sagepub.com/doi/10.1177/0956797613499592

2. https://www.ncbi.nlm.nih.gov/pmc/articles/PMC6091269/

3. https://www.ncbi.nlm.nih.gov/pmc/articles/PMC4417099/

Chapter Four

Unclutter Your Sh**

We can describe decluttering as akin to peeling back the layers of chaos that surround us daily. It extends beyond arranging objects; it's a profound strategy that promises to streamline your existence, cut through the noise, and carve out space for tangible clarity. The art of decluttering unfolds as a multi-faceted approach, where the rewards reach far beyond the surface level. From heightened organization and enhanced productivity to the profound satisfaction of dwelling in a serene environment, the benefits are diverse and impactful.

To dive deeper into the transformative power of decluttering, we'll explore its various dimensions: physical, digital, mental, and emotional. Each facet contributes uniquely to the overarching goal of simplification. As we progress through these sections, we will dissect the distinctive advantages offered by each decluttering strategy.

The decluttering process isn't a one-size-fits-all endeavor. It's a tailored approach, and our objective is to equip you with hands-on tips and techniques that resonate with each type of decluttering. Whether you're decluttering your physical space, tidying up your digital presence, alleviating your mental luggage, or navigating your emotions, we aim to provide actionable insights.

Organize Your Space

Start small, and focus on one area at a time. The key is to prevent overwhelm. It could be your desk, a corner of your living room, or even just a shelf. As you do it, consider what items belong there and what can find a better home elsewhere.

Regularity is the name of the game. Make decluttering a part of your routine. Whether it's a few minutes each day or a designated time each week, consistency is crucial. This habit prevents the buildup of unnecessary items and keeps your space in a perpetual state of order.

This simple practice eliminates the frustrating search for misplaced keys or important documents. When everything has a designated spot, finding what you need becomes second nature, and it will reduce confusion and stress.

Minimalism

Adopting a minimalist mindset doesn't mean you have to transform into a Zen master overnight. Start by focusing on the essentials. Consider each item's utility and emotional value. If something doesn't serve a purpose or bring you joy, it might be time to bid it farewell.

Clear surfaces are your allies. Visual clutter can overwhelm your mind, making it challenging to concentrate and remember important details. By minimizing what's on display, you create a calmer visual environment that supports mental clarity.

Practicality Over Perfection

Functionality takes precedence over achieving a picture-perfect space. The goal is to create an environment that works for you and your daily activities. Consider how you use each space and organize it accordingly.

Flexibility is key. Your life is dynamic, and your surroundings should adapt. If a particular organization method isn't working, don't hesitate to tweak or overhaul it. The key is to create a system that suits your needs and evolves with you.

The Continuous Process

Decluttering isn't a one-and-done deal; it's an ongoing process. Embrace it as a lifestyle rather than a sporadic activity. Regularly assess your surroundings, asking yourself if items still serve a purpose or if they've become redundant.

As you engage in this process, you're not just tidying up physical space; you're cultivating a mental sanctuary. A clutter-free environment translates to a clutter-free mind. Your brain can focus more efficiently when it's not bombarded by the visual and mental noise of disorganization.

Digital Decluttering

Digital decluttering is about creating a digital environment that complements your mental clarity. It's a proactive approach to managing the overwhelming influx of information in the digital age. From managing files and emails to decluttering your device, we focus on practical steps to organize and simplify your digital spaces. This will allow you to regain control over your digital environment and promote a more efficient, focused, and stress-free digital experience.

Organize Digital Files

Your digital life can be a constant struggle for your attention and focus. Start by organizing your digital files just as you would with your physical space. Create folders with clear, intuitive names, and categorize your documents logically. A well-organized digital filing system ensures that you can swiftly locate what you need.

Consider implementing a routine for digital decluttering. Set aside time each week to sift through your files, delete duplicates, and organize new additions. Regular maintenance prevents the digital chaos from spiraling out of control and saves you from the frustration of searching through a cluttered desktop or chaotic folder structure.

Unsubscribe and Unfollow

Your inbox and social media feeds can easily become overwhelmed with information that adds little value to your life. Take charge by unsubscribing from newsletters that no longer interest you and unfollowing social media accounts that don't contribute positively to your well-being.

Reducing the digital noise not only streamlines your online experience but also frees up mental space. When you open your email or scroll through social media, you'll be met with content that matters, making your digital interactions more purposeful and less draining.

Scheduled Digital Breaks

Consider incorporating scheduled digital breaks into your day. Constant connectivity can contribute to mental fatigue. Designate specific times when you disconnect from digital devices, and allow your mind to recharge.

Password Management

Managing a multitude of passwords can be a headache. Simplify your digital life by using a reliable password manager. Not only does this enhance security, but it also reduces the mental burden of remembering numerous login credentials.

Mental Decluttering

Reducing cognitive load is about working smarter, not harder. By adopting strategies to streamline information, prioritize tasks, and make mindful decisions, you free up mental space for what truly matters. So, take a moment, assess your cognitive load, and implement these strategies to optimize your mental performance. Your brain will thank you with sharper focus and enhanced memory.

Organized Information

One key aspect of reducing cognitive load is organizing information. Break complex information into smaller, more manageable components. Whether it's a project at work or a personal goal, compartmentalizing information makes it easier for your brain to process and prioritize.

By providing your brain with a clear structure, you reduce the cognitive burden of uncertainty and ambiguity. This organized approach enhances not only your efficiency but also your overall mental clarity.

Prioritize Tasks

Your mind is likely full of tasks, commitments, and ideas. Take the chaos and turn it into a structured to-do list. Prioritize tasks based on urgency and importance. This simple act of organization not only ensures that nothing falls through the cracks but also prevents decision fatigue.

Break large tasks into smaller, more manageable steps. This makes them less daunting and provides a clear roadmap for execution. As you check off completed tasks, you'll experience a sense of accomplishment, reinforcing the positive impact on your productivity and mental well-being.

Delegate

Don't hesitate to delegate. You don't have to carry the weight of the world on your shoulders. Delegating tasks distributes the cognitive load, allowing you to focus on what truly requires your attention. It's not a sign of weakness but a smart strategy for optimizing your mental resources.

Single-tasking

In a world that glorifies multitasking, single-tasking is your best friend. Focus on one task at a time, fully immersing yourself in the present moment. This enhances the quality of your work and reduces mental clutter associated with juggling multiple tasks simultaneously. That way, you're empowering your mind to function with precision and purpose.

Repetition and Spaced Learning

Repetition and spaced learning—an educational method where learning material is reviewed over a prolonged period of time, with breaks or intervals in between—contribute to mental focus and prevent cognitive overload, which aligns with the goal of a clutter-free mind. These techniques involve methodical reinforcement, ensuring that information is revisited at intervals. This approach avoids the mental strain associated with cramming and promotes sustained focus.

Mnemonics and Creative Organization

Mnemonics inject a creative element into mental organization. Creating acronyms, rhymes, or sentences to remember information adds a touch of innovation to memory enhancement. This creativity not only aids in recall but also contributes to a mental environment that is both organized and engaging.

Journaling

Set aside dedicated time each day or week to unload your thoughts onto paper. You don't necessarily have to craft eloquent prose; it's about freeing your mind from the weight of unprocessed information. As you put pen to paper, let your thoughts flow without judgment. Jot down tasks, ideas, worries, or anything occupying your mind. The act of externalizing these thoughts allows your brain to release them, creating mental space for more important matters.

Regular Reflection

Make this a recurring practice, a ritual of reflection. Regularly revisit your journal entries to assess your progress, identify recurring themes, and adjust your priorities accordingly. Reflection is not just about looking back; it's about looking forward with intention. Use your journal as a tool for goal setting, tracking personal growth, and refining your focus. This is a dynamic process that evolves with you and ensures its continual relevance to your life.

Regular Breaks

Your brain needs moments of rest to perform at its best. Schedule regular breaks to recharge. Engage in activities that bring joy and relaxation. Whether it's a short walk or deep breathing exercises, these breaks reduce cognitive load and enhance your overall cognitive resilience.

Emotional Declutter

In the pursuit of mental well-being, emotional decluttering is a transformative process. It's about creating a space within yourself that nurtures positive emotions and releases the grip of negativity. As you embrace practices like letting go, setting boundaries, and gratitude, you pave the way for a lighter, more emotionally resilient mind. These practical techniques will also help you handle stress and build resilience.

Letting Go

Emotional clutter is the accumulation of unresolved emotions, lingering grudges, and unnecessary worries. The first step in emotional decluttering is learning the art of letting go. Release the emotional baggage that no longer serves you, whether it's a past grievance, regret, or resentment.

Express Yourself

Bottling up emotions contributes to mental clutter. Find healthy outlets to express your feelings. This could be through talking to a trusted friend or therapist or engaging in creative activities. By giving voice to your emotions, you prevent them from festering and gaining unnecessary control over your mental state.

Mindfulness

Mindfulness is a powerful tool for emotional decluttering. It involves being present in the moment without judgment. Engaging in mindfulness will calm the mind and help you observe and detach from emotional clutter, which allows a more balanced and resilient emotional state.

Gratitude

Shift your focus from what's lacking to what you have. Cultivate a gratitude practice by regularly acknowledging and appreciating the positive aspects of your life. This simple act reframes your mindset, reducing negativity and emotional clutter. Gratitude must come from a genuine place. When it's done this way, it will naturally have a positive impact on your emotional state.

Forgiveness

Harboring resentment is a significant source of emotional clutter. Practice forgiveness, not only for others but for yourself. Letting go of grudges frees your mind from the weight of negative emotions. It's a conscious decision to move forward without carrying the heavy baggage of past grievances.

Reflect and Release

Regularly reflect on your emotions and identify patterns of negativity. This self-awareness is a crucial step in emotional decluttering. Once you recognize emotional clutter, consciously release it. This may involve affirmations, visualization, or simply acknowledging and accepting the emotion without judgment.

Social Declutter

Social decluttering means taking a closer look at your social circles to boost your overall well-being. It's like moving through a collection of connections, keeping the ones that add value and letting go of those that bring unnecessary noise.

Evaluate Relationships

Reflecting on your friendships is like taking a compass to your social world. Start by creating a mental or written inventory of your connections. Identify those that genuinely bring joy, support, and positive energy into your life. Gauge the impact each connection has on your mental and emotional well-being. It's about surrounding yourself with those who contribute positively to your life.

Cultivate Meaningful Connections

Imagine your social life as a garden; focus on nurturing a select few relationships, cultivating them with care and attention. Instead of spreading yourself thin, invest time and energy in the connections that resonate most with your values and aspirations. These genuine, meaningful relationships act as anchors, providing a solid foundation for your overall well-being.

Schedule Quality Time

Actively planning quality time with significant people in your life is like putting deposits into your emotional bank. It could be as simple as a coffee date, a heart-to-heart phone call, or engaging in activities that strengthen your bond. Prioritize these moments, making them a non-negotiable part of your schedule. By doing so, you're developing a deeper connection and creating memories that contribute positively to your overall sense of happiness.

Join Groups with Shared Interests

Join groups or activities aligned with your interests, and open doors to new connections. Seek out communities that resonate with your passions – it could be a book club, a hiking group, or a painting class. By engaging in activities you genuinely enjoy, you're more likely to meet like-minded individuals. These shared interests become the foundation for authentic connections, offering a chance to expand your social circle with people who understand and appreciate your passions.

Set Boundaries

Emotional clutter often arises from unhealthy relationships or unrealistic expectations. Establish clear boundaries to protect your emotional well-being. Learn to say no when needed and prioritize your mental health. Creating space for positive, supportive relationships and minimizing exposure to toxic influences is crucial.

Financial Decluttering

Financial decluttering involves simplifying and organizing one's financial life for greater peace of mind.

Budget Like a Pro

Creating a budget is about taking control of your financial narrative. Begin by jotting down your monthly income and essential expenses. Then, set realistic goals for discretionary spending. Keep a close eye on where your money goes, and adjust your budget as needed. Tracking expenses empowers you to make informed financial decisions, paving the way for a stress-free and stable financial future.

Keep It Simple

Financial peace thrives in simplicity. Consolidate your financial accounts to streamline your money management. Automate recurring payments to avoid late fees and reduce the mental load of constant bill tracking. By simplifying your financial responsibilities, you open up mental space to focus on what truly matters: your well-being.

Ditch That Debt

Tackling debt can be daunting, but it's your ticket to financial freedom. Start by listing all your debts, from credit cards to loans. Create a repayment plan, prioritizing high-interest debts first. Look for opportunities to negotiate interest rates or consolidate debts. As you chip away at your debts, you'll feel the burden lifting, bringing you one step closer to financial independence and peace of mind.

Invest in You

Shift your perspective on spending. Instead of accumulating possessions, redirect your resources toward experiences, education, and health. Invest in activities that bring you joy and personal growth. Consider allocating funds for a course you've been eyeing, a trip that broadens your horizons, or activities that contribute to your mental and physical well-being. Remember, true wealth lies not just in possessions but in a life rich with meaningful experiences and continuous self-improvement.

Routine and Habits

To boost mental clarity and memory, stick to routines—they're your best allies. A well-structured routine provides a sense of stability and predictability, reducing decision fatigue and freeing up mental space for more important tasks.

Your Brain Loves Patterns

The brain thrives on patterns and repetition. Routines and habits create neural pathways that signal to your brain what to expect and when. This predictability reduces the cognitive load associated with constant decision-making, creating a more streamlined mental environment.

In the world of memory enhancement and mental well-being, routines and habits are very important. They provide the structure your brain craves, promoting efficiency and reducing unnecessary stress. As you weave these practices into your daily life, you're not just establishing routines; you're nurturing a mental landscape primed for optimal performance and a sharper memory. So, embrace the power of routines and habits; your mind will thank you with increased focus and enhanced cognitive function.

Building Habits

Habits are the building blocks of a well-structured routine. Identify habits that align with your goals and contribute to mental well-being. Whether it's a daily exercise routine, a habit of reading before bed, or a consistent hydration ritual, these habits become automatic, reducing the cognitive load associated with decision-making.

Morning Rituals

Begin your day with purposeful morning rituals. These can include activities like meditation, stretching, or a nutritious breakfast. A consistent morning routine sets a positive tone for the day, and signals to your brain that it's time to shift into focused and productive mode.

Consistent Sleep Patterns

Quality sleep is a crucial factor when it comes to mental well-being and memory consolidation. Establish a consistent sleep routine by going to bed and waking up at the same time each day. Prioritize sleep hygiene, and create a conducive environment for restful nights. The result is a more alert and focused mind during waking hours.

Reflective Evening Routine

Cap off your day with a reflective evening routine. Take a few minutes to review your accomplishments, express gratitude, and plan for the next day. This practice not only promotes a positive mindset but also prepares your brain for a restful night's sleep.

Adaptability in Routine

While routines provide stability, it's essential to remain adaptable. Life is dynamic, and flexibility in your routine is key to navigating unexpected challenges. The ability to adapt your routine allows for continued mental resilience and prevents unnecessary stress when faced with disruptions.

Conclusion

We have discussed physical, digital, mental, and emotional decluttering. Now you understand that this goes way beyond tidying up; it's about reclaiming control and finding tranquility in simplicity.

Physically, we've tossed out the excess, making space for what truly matters. Digitally, we've cut through the digital noise, leaving room for clarity in our virtual realms. Mentally, we've sorted through the mental clutter, making way for sharper focus and purpose. Emotionally, we've let go of the unnecessary baggage, paving the way for emotional well-being.

Decluttering isn't a one-time event; it's a mindset. It's about consistently assessing what adds value and shedding what doesn't. So, whether it's the tangible items in your home, the digital files on your devices, the thoughts in your mind, or the emotions in your heart, embrace the practice of decluttering. Your space, your mind, and your heart will thank you.

Chapter Five

Get Some Sleep and Stop Eating Bad Sh**

In this chapter, we'll explore two often underestimated but crucial elements in our pursuit of enhanced cognitive abilities: sleep and nutrition. These are the silent architects shaping our mental resilience and determining our capacity to conquer daily challenges.

First, we'll dive into the importance of sleep, a restorative sanctuary where our minds rejuvenate and memories solidify. Beyond its role in alleviating fatigue, sleep stands as an indispensable factor in memory consolidation and cognitive rejuvenation and is often overshadowed by the bustling demands of our daily lives.

Then, we'll emphasize the role of nutrition, unraveling the symbiotic relationship between our dietary choices and cognitive performance. Food is way more than just a fuel for our bodies; it has tremendous effects on our mental aspects. With a focus on scientifically-backed strategies, we'll explore the importance of nutrients like antioxidants, omega-3 fatty acids, and other essential vitamins for our mental acuity.

This exploration is grounded in practicality, offering valuable insights into optimizing sleep patterns and making informed dietary decisions. No gimmicks, no elusive promises—just a pragmatic journey to empower you with the knowledge to take control of your cognitive destiny. It's time to acknowledge the significance of these foundational elements, setting the stage for a sharper mind and a more accomplished version of yourself.

Understanding Sleep

When we explore the mystery of sleep, we find ourselves delving into the dynamics of the brain's internal warfare—a relentless conflict between two opposing forces, the circadian arousal system ("process C") and the homeostatic sleep drive ("process S"). This struggle unfolds not in mere nightly episodes but as a ceaseless battle throughout our waking and sleeping moments, creating a cyclical rhythm in our daily lives.

Contrary to the common assumption that sleep equates to the brain's rest, research reveals an astonishing level of activity during "rest." Neurons communicate vigorously, orchestrating intricate electrical commands in constantly shifting patterns. The brain, far from dormant, exhibits heightened rhythmic activity during sleep, surpassing that seen when wide awake. It challenges our traditional understanding, prompting a reevaluation of the purpose of rest in the first place.

However, amid this apparent contradiction, we can perceive a fundamental idea: true rest for the brain occurs in the deepest phases of non-REM sleep, which constitutes a mere 20% of the total sleep cycle. This challenges the simplistic notion that sleep is primarily about providing rest to the brain.

The paradox deepens when we acknowledge the vulnerability sleep introduces. In a state of vulnerability akin to a human version of micro-hibernation, we willingly surrender to a state where predators, both real and imagined, could pose a threat. This raises an essential question: What compels us to risk such vulnerability?

The pioneering work of sleep researcher William C. Dement sheds light on this enigma. Sleep, it appears, is not a tranquil respite but a battleground. The opponent-process model he introduced portrays the ongoing war between the circadian arousal system and the homeostatic sleep drive. These powerful armies composed of neurons, hormones, and biochemicals engage in daily warfare, each seeking dominance but never achieving final victory.

This continuous conflict, with its peculiar win/loss cycle, results in the ebb and flow of waking and sleeping experiences. The circadian arousal system relentlessly drives wakefulness, while the homeostatic sleep drive strives for rest. Neither claims ultimate triumph; instead, they orchestrate a predictable cycle governed by internal clocks, regulated by brain regions like the suprachiasmatic nucleus.

The duration and intensity of sleep are maintained by "process S," ensuring a necessary respite, while "process C" dictates the propensity and timing for wakefulness. It is an intricate dance between these internal forces, a dance regulated by external factors like chronotype and the nap zone.

This exploration extends beyond the theoretical and invites us to understand the practical implications of this internal struggle. By recognizing that our daily rhythm is a result of these opposing forces, we gain insight into managing our sleep effectively. Our internal clocks, just like a complex mechanism, demand attention and understanding.

What Kind of Sleeper Are You?

Exploring sleep patterns and chronotypes shows a captivating panorama of individuality and complexity. In a society shaped by routines and expectations, the classifications of "early risers," "night owls," and "flexible sleepers" shed light on the diverse ways individuals harmonize with their internal biological clocks.

Take, for instance, Ann Landers, the acclaimed advice columnist, who resolutely protected her sleep time by disconnecting her phone between 1 and 10 a.m. Her steadfast commitment to her circadian rhythm exemplified a profound understanding of the consequences of aligning one's activities with their unique sleep-wake cycle. Conversely, consider Scott Adams, the creator of Dilbert, embodying the productivity of an early riser by crafting his comic strip from 6 to 7 a.m. His deliberate synchronization with his creative rhythms underscores the variety of approaches individuals employ to optimize their cognitive functioning.

The categorization of individuals as early risers, night owls, or flexible sleepers provides a framework for understanding the spectrum of sleep preferences. Early risers, constituting about one in ten individuals, effortlessly wake before alarms, reporting peak alertness around noon. In contrast, night owls, encompassing two in ten people, find their productivity peak in the late evening, seldom retiring before 3:00 AM. The majority, termed flexible sleepers, encompass a spectrum of preferences, incorporating elements of both early risers and night owls.

The genetic origins of these chronotypes reveal obvious familial patterns. The influence of parental sleep preferences on their children's patterns demonstrates the hereditary nature of these sleep-wake cycles. Early risers tend to pass down their tendencies, contributing to the perpetuation of distinct sleep-wake cycles across generations.

However, the concept of flexible sleepers challenges the dichotomy of early risers and night owls. Representing the majority of the population, flexible sleepers embody the fluidity and individuality inherent in sleep preferences. Some lean towards early-rising tendencies while others align more with night-owl behaviors. This spectrum of preferences reinforces the idea that sleep patterns are not rigidly predetermined but rather malleable and influenced by various factors.

A paradigm shift emerges when we question the traditional idea of a universally recommended duration of sleep. Rather than presenting a conclusive response to the inquiry of how much sleep one needs, we underscore the extraordinary individuality of sleep requirements. The ever-changing nature of sleep patterns adds complexity with variables such as age, gender, pregnancy, and puberty molding one's sleep-wake cycle.

Of utmost importance is the recognition that dysfunctionality can stem from both excess and insufficiency in sleep. This challenges the prevalent notion that increased sleep directly correlates with improved well-being. The delicate equilibrium between too much and too little sleep unveils the intricate interplay between sleep and cognitive function. This revelation serves as a cautionary note, urging readers to reassess their presumptions regarding the volume of sleep essential for optimal brain health.

In conclusion, the exploration of sleep patterns and chronotypes offers a profound understanding of the diversity inherent in human experiences of wakefulness and rest. By recognizing the individuality and genetic influences on sleep preferences, individuals can tailor their routines to align with their unique chronotypes. This nuanced approach promotes a deeper appreciation for the relation between biology and behavior and allows individuals to optimize their cognitive well-being through informed decisions about their sleep habits.

Impacts of Lack of Sleep

Learning

Lack of sleep is a formidable adversary to effective learning, capable of setting even the most successful students on a precarious academic decline. A study indicates that a high-achieving student accustomed to scoring in the top 10% may plummet to the bottom 9% with just under seven hours of sleep on weekdays. The cumulative losses throughout the week translate into deficits during the weekend, creating a sleep debt that spills over into the subsequent week. This revelation underscores the critical role of consistent, quality sleep in maintaining cognitive prowess and academic success.

Physiology

Sleep deprivation has a pervasive impact on cognitive functions. Beyond impairing learning, it extends to compromising the body's ability to utilize food, diminishing insulin production, and triggering an increased demand for food due to rising stress hormone levels. The body's physiological response to sleep deprivation is positioned as a critical factor in understanding the interconnectedness of sleep, cognitive functions, and overall well-being.

Aging

There is a correlation between the accelerated aging processes and sleep loss. Studies have shown that sleep-deprived thirty-year-olds body chemistry will regress to that of a sixty-year-old within six days of insufficient sleep. The delayed recovery to a youthful state underscores the lasting consequences of sleep deprivation, which proves the toll it takes not only on cognitive functions but on overall physiological well-being.

Thinking

Sleep loss has many repercussions on various dimensions of thinking. Attention, executive function, memory (both immediate and working), mood, quantitative skills, logical reasoning, and general mathematical knowledge all fall prey to the insidious effects of sleep deprivation.

Compromised sleep jeopardizes cognitive abilities across the spectrum, and prioritizing sleep is crucial for the preservation of mental acuity.

Memory

A study involving rats showcases a distinct pattern of electrical activity in the brain as they learn a maze. The findings reveal that during sleep, these rats engage in the replay of the acquired pattern, hinting at a process akin to memory consolidation. Intriguingly, when the sleep cycle is disrupted precisely during this phase, the rats experience difficulty recalling the maze. This underscores the critical role of uninterrupted sleep in facilitating effective learning.

Analogous to the rat's experience, humans seem to replay specific daily learning encounters at night, particularly during the slow-wave phase, which is crucial to memory consolidation. Diverging from the rat, emotionally charged memories replay at a distinct stage in the sleep cycle. These revelations propose a groundbreaking idea: offline processing occurs during the night. Sleep serves as a mechanism to redirect attentional resources inward for deep cognitive processing.

Improve Your Sleep

Let's discuss evidence-based insights and actionable tips to reclaim rejuvenating nights. We will explore sleep hygiene, consistent schedules, optimal environments, and pre-sleep rituals, demystifying the science behind quality sleep. We're here to empower you with practical tools, debunk myths, and usher in a transformative approach to nightly repose. Whether you seek occasional solutions or a complete sleep overhaul, this guide is your companion to a healthier, more vibrant life through improved sleep. Join us on the journey to profound rest and well-being.

Stick to Your Sleep Schedule

Consistency is the cornerstone of cultivating healthy sleep habits, and maintaining a regular sleep schedule stands as a linchpin in the pursuit of optimal rest. The human body, deeply tuned to the rhythms of day and night, thrives on predictability when it comes to sleep-wake cycles. Here, we delve into the profound impact of sticking to a designated sleep schedule and how this steadfast routine can significantly elevate the quality of your sleep.

A consistent sleep schedule involves going to bed and waking up at the same time every day, even on weekends. This may seem deceptively simple, but the body's internal clock, known as the circadian rhythm, responds favorably to routine. When bedtime and wake-up time remain steady, the circadian rhythm synchronizes with these cues, optimizing the natural ebb and flow of sleep-inducing hormones.

Why does this matter? The circadian rhythm regulates a myriad of physiological processes, including body temperature, hormone release, and sleep-wake transitions. When we disrupt this delicate balance with irregular sleep patterns, we jeopardize the body's ability to anticipate and respond to the need for rest. Inconsistent sleep schedules can lead to difficulties falling asleep, frequent awakenings during the night, and a sense of grogginess upon waking.

Start by determining a bedtime that allows for the recommended amount of sleep for your age group. Then, work backward to create a winding-down routine that begins about thirty minutes before you plan to sleep.

During this pre-sleep phase, engage in calming activities that signal to your body that it's time to unwind. This might include reading a book, practicing relaxation techniques, or listening to soothing music.

Additionally, ensure your sleep environment is conducive to rest by keeping it cool, dark, and quiet.

Consistency, however, extends beyond bedtime and permeates into the morning. Strive to wake up at the same time every day, even on weekends. This reinforces the synchronicity of your body's internal clock, fostering a robust and reliable sleep-wake pattern.

Reduce Lights Before Bedtime

In order to have a restful night's sleep, one often overlooked yet vital element is the management of light in the hours leading up to bedtime. As the evening unfolds and the day gradually retreats into darkness, the type and intensity of lighting in our surroundings play a pivotal role in signaling the body that it's time to transition from wakefulness to rest.

Modern lifestyles are often dominated by artificial lighting, from the soft glow of screens to the harsh glare of overhead bulbs. However, this pervasive exposure to bright light, particularly the blue light emitted by electronic devices, can interfere with the body's natural circadian rhythm. The circadian rhythm, often referred to as the body's internal clock, regulates the sleep-wake cycle and is highly responsive to changes in light.

Reducing exposure to bright or blue-enriched light sources in the hour or two before bedtime is a practical and scientifically supported strategy for promoting better sleep. The reasoning behind this approach lies in the impact of light on the production of melatonin, a hormone crucial for regulating sleep. The body typically begins to release melatonin as daylight diminishes, signaling the onset of the sleep phase.

The pervasive presence of artificial light, especially in the evening, can suppress melatonin production, sending mixed signals to the body about the appropriate time to wind down. Consequently, individuals may find it challenging to fall asleep promptly or experience a diminished quality of sleep.

To integrate this knowledge into your sleep routine, consider adopting a gradual reduction of light as bedtime approaches. Begin by switching to softer, warmer-hued lighting in the evening, avoiding the harsh brilliance of cool-toned bulbs. Dim the lights in your living space as bedtime nears, creating a calm and subdued ambiance that aligns with your body's natural sleep cues.

Furthermore, limit exposure to screens emitting blue light, such as phones, tablets, and computers, at least an hour before sleep. The blue light from these devices can suppress melatonin production, hindering the body's ability to prepare for a restful night.

Don't Worry or Plan Before Bedtime

Engaging in worry or extensive planning during the pre-sleep hours can act as a disruptor, preventing the mind from transitioning into a calm state conducive to sleep. When the brain is preoccupied with thoughts of the day's challenges or tomorrow's tasks, the body remains in a heightened state of alertness, making it challenging to embrace the restorative sleep the night promises.

To promote a peaceful pre-sleep routine, consider designating a specific period in the evening for contemplation and planning. This distinct timeframe, ideally well before bedtime, allows you to address concerns or organize thoughts without encroaching on the sacred moments leading up to sleep. By compartmentalizing these activities, you create a mental boundary that shields the tranquility needed for rest.

A practical strategy involves jotting down concerns or plans in a dedicated journal. This not only provides a tangible outlet for your thoughts but also frees the mind from the burden of carrying these considerations into the bedroom. The act of transferring worries onto paper can be a cathartic release, allowing the mind to relinquish its grip on these concerns as you prepare to sleep.

Another effective approach is to engage in relaxation techniques before bedtime. Practices such as deep breathing and meditation serve to calm the nervous system, signaling to the body that it's time to unwind. The deliberate focus on the present moment during these activities helps redirect the mind away from future worries, which fosters a serene mental environment conducive to sleep.

By minimizing worrying or planning during the pre-sleep hours, individuals pave the way for a more tranquil transition into the realm of sleep, which unlocks the full rejuvenating potential of the night.

The Bedroom Is Only for Sleep

The bedroom, ideally, should be a haven where the mind and body seamlessly transition into a state of restfulness. The pervasive trend of converting bedrooms into multifunctional areas for work, entertainment, or exercise disrupts this delicate balance. Designating the bedroom as a dedicated sleep space devoid of work-related materials or electronic gadgets sends a powerful signal to the brain: it's time for rejuvenation.

One critical facet of this approach involves refraining from bringing work-related stressors into the bedroom. The intrusion of professional concerns, facilitated by the omnipresence of digital devices, can hinder the brain's ability to unwind and prepare for sleep. By keeping the bedroom free from work-related distractions, individuals establish a clear demarcation between the demands of the day and the serenity required for a good night's sleep.

Similarly, transforming the bedroom into an entertainment hub with televisions, gaming consoles, or other electronic gadgets can disrupt the tranquility necessary for quality sleep. The artificial light emitted by screens interferes with the body's natural circadian rhythm, negatively impacting the production of melatonin, the hormone crucial for regulating sleep-wake cycles.

A purposefully curated bedroom stripped of unnecessary diversions serves as a dedicated space for sleep preparation. This intentional focus aids in conditioning the mind, reinforcing the association between the bedroom and restful activities. By respecting the singular purpose of the bedroom—sleep—individuals pave the way for creating an environment that aligns with the body's innate sleep-wake rhythm.

Importance of Uninterrupted Sleep

The human sleep cycle consists of distinct stages, each serving a unique purpose in maintaining overall well-being. The interruption of this seamless progression, whether by external disturbances or fragmented sleep patterns, jeopardizes the integrity of these stages. The consequences extend beyond mere drowsiness, delving into the intricacies of cognitive function, emotional resilience, and physical vitality.

Uninterrupted sleep allows the body to traverse the intricate landscape of rapid eye movement (REM) and non-REM sleep cycles without disruption. During REM sleep, vital cognitive functions such as memory consolidation and emotional regulation unfold, contributing significantly to mental acuity and resilience. The non-REM phases, marked by slow-wave sleep, focus on physical restoration, bolstering immune function, and facilitating the repair of tissues and muscles.

Disruptions to this rhythmic progression, often induced by external noises, stressors, or sleep disorders, fragment the harmonious orchestration of these sleep cycles. Such interruptions not only compromise the depth and quality of rest but also impede the body's ability to perform essential reparative processes.

Recognizing the importance of uninterrupted sleep underscores the commitment to prioritizing one's overall health and well-being. It transcends the conventional notion of sleep duration, emphasizing the qualitative aspect of rest as a cornerstone for physical and mental vitality. The quest for uninterrupted sleep, therefore, necessitates a conscious cultivation of an environment conducive to tranquility and an adequate management of stressors.

Establish a Relaxing Pre-Sleep Routine

The moments preceding sleep provide a valuable window for setting the stage for a restful night. Crafting a calming pre-sleep routine is akin to laying the groundwork for a serene transition from wakefulness to slumber. In bustling lives marked by incessant digital engagement and demanding schedules, the importance of cultivating a tranquil pre-sleep ritual cannot be overstated.

Embracing activities that promote relaxation becomes instrumental. Reading, preferably in the gentle embrace of dim light, serves as a gentle departure from the day's commotion. The choice of reading material should veer away from stimulating or suspenseful narratives and lean more toward content that soothes the mind. Whether it's a calming novel, poetry, or non-fiction with a serene tone, the aim is to facilitate a gradual mental unwinding.

The environment in which this pre-sleep ritual unfolds plays a pivotal role. Creating a cool, dark, and quiet sleep sanctuary reinforces the body's natural inclination to unwind. Drawing the curtains, adjusting the room temperature, and minimizing ambient noise contribute to this cocoon of calmness.

In essence, cultivating a relaxing pre-sleep routine is about orchestrating a symphony of elements that guide the mind and body gently toward the shores of sleep. By conscientiously curating these pre-sleep moments, one not only acknowledges the necessity of rest but actively participates in preparing the mind and body for a rejuvenating night's sleep.

Short Naps

One of the key advantages of napping lies in its ability to combat the notorious midday slump. The circadian rhythm naturally includes a dip in alertness and energy levels during the afternoon, commonly known as the post-lunch dip. Rather than pushing through this period with caffeine or sheer willpower, a well-timed nap can serve as a strategic intervention. A brief nap of around twenty to thirty minutes has been shown to enhance alertness and performance, offering a mental refresh without the grogginess associated with longer naps.

Moreover, napping has a remarkable impact on memory and learning. Research suggests that a short nap can improve memory consolidation, aiding in the retention of newly acquired information. Whether you're a student preparing for exams or a professional tackling a steep learning curve, incorporating a nap into your routine can provide a cognitive boost, helping you grasp and retain complex concepts more effectively.

Beyond the immediate cognitive benefits, napping contributes to emotional well-being. A well-timed nap acts as a rejuvenating break, offering a reset for the mind and a chance to alleviate stress. This emotional recharge can enhance resilience and contribute to a more positive mental state.

Diet and Cognitive Function

The connection between diet and cognitive function is a multifaceted and dynamic relationship that underscores the profound impact of our dietary choices on the health of our brains. As the epicenter of cognitive processes, memory, and overall mental well-being, the brain is intricately influenced by the nutrients it receives from the foods we consume.

Nutrient-Rich Foods

A diet rich in essential nutrients, including vitamins, minerals, antioxidants, and omega-3 fatty acids, is associated with optimal cognitive function. These nutrients play key roles in neuronal function, neurotransmitter synthesis, and protection against oxidative stress. Foods such as fruits, vegetables, whole grains, fish, and nuts contribute to a nutrient-rich diet that supports overall brain health.

Antioxidants

Antioxidants, abundant in colorful fruits and vegetables, play a crucial role in combating oxidative stress. The brain is particularly susceptible to oxidative damage due to its high metabolic rate and significant lipid content. Including antioxidant-rich foods in the diet helps protect brain cells from free radical damage, fostering an environment conducive to sustained cognitive function.

Omega-3 Fatty Acids

Omega-3 fatty acids, predominantly found in fatty fish, flaxseeds, and walnuts, are integral to the structural integrity of brain cell membranes. These fatty acids contribute to efficient neural communication, support synaptic plasticity, and may play a role in mitigating inflammation.

Including sources of omega-3s in the diet has been associated with better cognitive performance and a lower risk of cognitive decline.

Blood Sugar Regulation

The stability of blood sugar levels is crucial for sustained cognitive function. Diets high in refined sugars and processed carbohydrates can lead to rapid spikes and crashes in blood glucose, impacting attention, concentration, and memory. A balanced diet that includes complex carbohydrates helps regulate blood sugar levels, providing a steady and reliable energy supply to the brain.

Gut-Brain Axis

The gut-brain axis, a bidirectional communication system between the gut and the brain, highlights the influence of the gut microbiome on cognitive function. A diet rich in fiber, prebiotics, and probiotics promotes a healthy gut microbiome, positively influencing neurotransmitter production and reducing inflammation. Emerging research suggests that an imbalance in gut bacteria may contribute to cognitive disorders, emphasizing the importance of dietary choices in maintaining gut health.

Protein and Amino Acids

Proteins, composed of essential amino acids, are fundamental to neurotransmitter synthesis. Amino acids derived from dietary proteins contribute to the production of neurotransmitters that regulate mood, memory, and cognitive processes. Including lean protein sources in the diet ensures an adequate supply of these building blocks, supporting optimal neurotransmitter function.

Hydration

Even mild dehydration can impair cognitive function, affecting attention, short-term memory, and mood. Adequate hydration facilitated by water-rich foods and proper fluid intake supports overall brain health by ensuring optimal blood flow and nutrient delivery to brain cells.

Understanding the connection between diet and cognitive function empowers individuals to make informed choices that support brain health throughout life. A balanced and varied diet, rich in nutrient-dense foods, not only nourishes the body but also provides the essential elements for maintaining cognitive vitality and mitigating the risk of cognitive decline.

Effects of a Poor Diet on Memory and Cognitive Function

Impaired Memory Formation

A diet laden with processed foods, saturated fats, and refined sugars can significantly impair memory formation. The consistent spikes and crashes in blood sugar levels associated with such dietary choices disrupt the intricate balance necessary for optimal brain function. The hippocampus, a key player in memory consolidation, becomes particularly vulnerable. Prolonged exposure to an unhealthy diet may compromise the hippocampus's structural integrity, hindering its ability to efficiently encode and retrieve memories. This interference in memory formation poses a substantial risk, especially as we age and the brain's resilience to such dietary insults diminishes.

Increased Oxidative Stress

The absence of antioxidant-rich foods in poor diets contributes to increased oxidative stress, posing a threat to cognitive health. Oxidative stress arises from an imbalance between free radicals and the body's ability to neutralize them. Without a sufficient supply of antioxidants from fruits, vegetables, and other nutrient-dense sources, the brain's defense mechanisms become overwhelmed. This heightened oxidative stress can lead to cellular damage, particularly affecting neurons critical for cognitive functions. The long-term repercussions may include accelerated cognitive decline, memory impairments, and an increased susceptibility to neurodegenerative conditions.

Inflammation and Cognitive Decline

Diets high in saturated fats and processed foods are known contributors to chronic inflammation, a condition with far-reaching implications for cognitive health. Inflammation within the brain disrupts the delicate balance required for efficient neuronal communication and functionality. The resulting environment is conducive to the accumulation of beta-amyloid plaques, infamous instigators of Alzheimer's disease. Prolonged exposure to an inflammatory diet elevates the risk of cognitive decline, as the immune system's responses may inadvertently damage the very brain cells crucial for memory and cognitive prowess.

Altered Neurotransmitter Function

The synthesis of neurotransmitters, the chemical messengers facilitating communication between neurons, relies heavily on essential nutrients, particularly B vitamins. Poor dietary choices devoid of these vital nutrients found in whole grains, lean meats, and leafy greens can disrupt this delicate balance. Imbalances in neurotransmitter levels may manifest as fluctuations in mood, compromised concentration, and impaired cognitive performance. Such alterations in neurotransmitter function not only impact day-to-day cognitive abilities but also contribute to long-term memory impairments.

Vascular Consequences

Unhealthy fats, characteristic of diets high in processed foods, contribute to the development of cardiovascular issues, including atherosclerosis. The compromised blood flow resulting from vascular damage has direct consequences for cognitive function. As arteries supplying the brain become restricted, oxygen and nutrient delivery to brain cells are compromised. This vascular insufficiency becomes a significant factor in memory loss and cognitive decline, emphasizing the intricate connection between vascular health and cognitive function.

Microbiome Imbalance

The intricate relationship between the gut and the brain, often referred to as the gut-brain axis, is a burgeoning area of research. Poor dietary choices, particularly those low in fiber and rich in processed foods, can disrupt the delicate balance of gut microbiota. The gut microbiome plays a pivotal role in regulating inflammation and producing compounds that influence brain function. An imbalanced microbiome has been associated with cognitive issues, making it imperative to recognize the impact of dietary habits on the microbial communities residing in our digestive system.

Insufficient Nutrient Intake

Beyond the spotlight on specific nutrients like omega-3 fatty acids and antioxidants, the overall nutritional content of one's diet is crucial for cognitive health. Insufficient intake of essential vitamins and minerals, such as vitamin D, which is vital for brain function, can contribute to cognitive decline. A diverse and well-rounded diet that includes a spectrum of nutrients from various food groups is essential to ensure the body receives the building blocks necessary for optimal cognitive function throughout life.

Dehydration

Even mild dehydration can exert adverse effects on cognitive function. Poor dietary choices, especially those characterized by high sodium intake and a lack of water-rich foods like fruits and vegetables, can contribute to insufficient hydration. Dehydration may impair concentration, increase feelings of fatigue, and hinder memory recall. Recognizing the importance of adequate fluid intake as part of a healthy diet becomes crucial in maintaining optimal cognitive performance.

Glycemic Control

Diets with a high glycemic index, often associated with refined carbohydrates like white bread and sugary snacks, can lead to rapid spikes and subsequent crashes in blood sugar levels. The resulting fluctuations can impair cognitive function, particularly in individuals susceptible to insulin resistance. Stable blood sugar levels are essential for sustained energy and cognitive vitality. Therefore, a focus on complex carbohydrates and balanced meals aids in maintaining glycemic control and supports overall brain health.

Neurotransmitter Regulation

The regulation of neurotransmitters, the chemical messengers influencing mood and cognitive function, relies on various amino acids derived from dietary proteins. Inadequate protein intake or an imbalance in amino acids can disrupt the synthesis of neurotransmitters, potentially affecting memory and cognitive processes. A diet that provides an adequate and balanced supply of protein from diverse sources is essential for supporting neurotransmitter function and maintaining optimal cognitive performance over time.

Understanding these additional factors emphasizes the intricate relationship between dietary choices and cognitive health. A holistic approach to brain well-being requires not only avoiding specific risks but also cultivating a diverse and nutrient-rich diet that supports the complex web of physiological processes essential for cognitive function. In summary, the consequences of poor dietary choices on memory and cognitive function extend beyond immediate concerns and delve into the intricate mechanisms of brain health. This underscores the necessity of adopting and maintaining a nutrient-rich diet for the preservation of cognitive abilities throughout the lifespan.

How to Improve Your Diet

Eat Memory-Boosting Foods

- **Dark Chocolate:** Delight in the taste of dark chocolate, which not only satisfies your sweet tooth but is also rich in antioxidants. These antioxidants play a protective role against free radicals, supporting learning and cognitive functions and potentially delaying the onset of Alzheimer's.

- **Beans:** Integrate beans into your meals for a nutrient-rich boost. Beans are laden with fiber, B vitamins, and omega fatty acids. Fiber facilitates prolonged satiety and a gradual release of sugar, contributing to enhanced concentration and memory. B vitamins play a role in converting homocysteine into crucial brain chemicals, such as acetylcholine, vital for memory creation. The omega fatty acids present are essential for both brain development and sustained function.

- **Red Wine:** Indulge in red wine in moderation, as it contains the antioxidant resveratrol. This compound enhances blood flow to the brain, supporting attention and concentration, with potential benefits in reducing the risk of Alzheimer's.

- **Whole Grains:** Opt for whole grains rich in complex carbohydrates, omega-3s, and B vitamins. These elements collectively support normal brain function, providing energy supply that regulates mood, and behavior and aids in learning and memory.

- **Salmon:** Opt for oily fish like salmon as it is a rich source of omega-3 fatty acids. It serves as a fundamental building block for the brain, enhancing overall cognitive function. Increased intake of omega-3 has demonstrated positive effects on the memory of individuals with Alzheimer's.

- **Avocados:** Enjoy the rich texture of avocados, packed with omega fatty acids and vitamin E. These essential nutrients contribute to cell growth, and brain development and protect cell membranes from free radicals. Vitamin E has the potential to slow degenerative diseases such as Alzheimer's.

- **Green Tea:** Savor the benefits of green tea, packed with antioxidants that protect against free radicals, which are unstable molecules that pose a threat to your body's cells.

- **Tomatoes:** Integrate tomatoes into your diet for their lycopene content, a potent antioxidant. Lycopene regulates genes influencing inflammation and controls cell growth within the brain, offering protective benefits.

- **Nuts and Seeds:** Incorporate nuts such as almonds, peanuts, and sunflower seeds into your diet. These brain-boosting foods are rich in protein and essential omega fatty acids. Protein, the second-largest component in the brain after water, plays a crucial role in fostering communication among neurons. Moreover, amino acids derived from proteins are vital for neurotransmitter production. Packed with omega-3 and omega-6 fatty acids, these nuts and seeds contribute essential fats that support cell construction, maintain normal brain function, and aid in memory formation through the creation of synapses.

- **Red Cabbage:** Try antioxidant-rich red cabbage, known for its ability to guard against free radicals that attack DNA, proteins, and carbohydrates in the body. The antioxidants present may contribute to countering the aging process and potentially play a role in Alzheimer's prevention.

- **Lean Red Meat:** Include lean red meats in your diet as they are rich in iron. Iron aids in neurotransmitter production and facilitates the transport of oxygen to the brain, supporting attention, concentration, and cognitive stimulation—a key factor in fending off Alzheimer's.

- **Blueberries:** Harness the power of antioxidants found in blueberries and other dark berries. These antioxidants act as protective shields against free radicals, promoting robust brain health. Moreover, they combat degenerative changes within the brain, fostering improved neural functioning and communication.

- **Quinoa:** Incorporate quinoa into your meals for its high content of complex carbs, iron, and B vitamins. Complex carbs serve as essential brain food, providing a steady energy supply crucial for normal brain function. Iron aids in blood oxygenation, contributing to attention and concentration, while B vitamins play a role in creating essential brain chemicals for memory formation.

- **Brown Rice:** Incorporate brown rice into your diet for its abundance of B-vitamins. These vitamins aid in converting homocysteine, an amino acid, into vital brain chemicals crucial for learning and memory formation.

- **Dark and Leafy Greens:** Incorporate greens like kale, spinach, and broccoli into your diet for their high vitamin E and folate content. Vitamin E safeguards cell membranes against free radicals, unstable molecules that attack cells within the body. Folate, also abundant in dark greens, supports normal brain development.

Incorporate Nutritious Foods Into Daily Meals

Embracing a brain-healthy diet doesn't necessitate a radical overhaul; instead, focus on gradual and sustainable changes. Begin by diversifying your meals with an array of colorful vegetables, whole grains, lean proteins, and healthy fats. Planning your meals ahead can foster consistency and allow for thoughtful choices. Opt for whole-grain alternatives to refined carbohydrates and adopt cooking methods that preserve nutritional integrity, such as grilling, baking, or steaming. Shift towards mindful snacking by choosing nutrient-dense options like nuts, seeds, or fresh fruit, steering clear of processed snacks. Substitute sugary beverages with hydrating choices like water, herbal teas, or infused water. Small, intentional adjustments in your daily food choices accumulate over time, forming the foundation of a sustainable and brain-healthy dietary pattern.

Meal Planning and Mindful Eating

To enhance your journey toward a brain-healthy diet, consider the strategic incorporation of meal planning, mindful eating, and informed food choices into your lifestyle. Meal planning empowers you to make intentional and nutritious choices, fostering consistency in your dietary habits. Dedicate a portion of your week to thoughtfully planning balanced meals, ensuring a diverse array of nutrients.

Embrace the practice of mindful eating by cultivating an awareness of your body's hunger and fullness signals. This approach encourages a more deliberate and satisfying dining experience, allowing you to appreciate the textures and flavors of your food. Additionally, prioritize informed food choices by scrutinizing labels and opting for whole, unprocessed options. This conscientious approach to selecting foods aligns with your cognitive well-being goals, steering you toward a sustainable and mindful relationship with nutrition.

Intermittent Fasting

Experiment with time-restricted eating, a practice often referred to as intermittent fasting. Our brains operate on glucose and ketones. During regular eating patterns, cells, including neurons, predominantly utilize glucose as their primary fuel. Fasting, characterized by an extended period without food intake, exhausts the liver's glucose stores. Consequently, the liver initiates the production of ketones, which are essentially fragments of fats that cells can efficiently utilize as an alternative energy source. This metabolic shift, transitioning from relying on glucose to utilizing ketones, typically occurs after a span of approximately ten to fourteen hours without food, contingent upon individual activity levels.

Fasting triggers the synthesis of a protein within nerve cells known as brain-derived neurotrophic factor (BDNF). This protein assumes pivotal roles in cognitive functions such as learning, memory, and the generation of new nerve cells. Beyond these functions, BDNF enhances neuronal resilience to stress, presenting an overall positive impact on brain health. Engaging in time-restricted eating could potentially leverage this metabolic switch to foster cognitive benefits associated with BDNF production.

Conclusion

In concluding the chapter, we find ourselves at the intersection of two critical pillars of cognitive well-being: sleep and nutrition.

Understanding the profound impact of quality sleep on various cognitive functions from memory to learning has emphasized the need for intentional sleep hygiene practices. Establishing a consistent sleep schedule, reducing pre-bedtime stimuli, and creating a tranquil sleep environment are pragmatic steps toward optimizing rest.

Simultaneously, our exploration into the intricate connection between diet and cognitive function underscores the significance of mindful food choices. Nutrient-rich foods, antioxidants, omega-3 fatty acids, and maintaining proper hydration emerge as pivotal elements in supporting cognitive health. The detrimental effects of a poor diet on memory and cognitive function underscore the urgency of adopting healthier dietary habits. Incorporating memory-boosting foods, embracing a balanced meal plan, and practicing mindful eating are actionable strategies to fortify cognitive resilience.

As we delve into the nexus of sleep and nutrition, the overarching message resonates: prioritizing these fundamental aspects is not merely a lifestyle choice but a profound investment in the vitality of our cognitive landscape, laying the groundwork for sustained mental acuity and overall well-being.

Chapter Six

Throw Out Sh** Habits

When we examine human behavior, "bad habits" appear to be subtle threads that, when left unexamined, can tightly weave themselves into our daily lives. These are seemingly innocuous routines that, unbeknownst to us, cast shadows on our productivity and over the clarity of our memory. The connection may not be immediately clear, but bad habits wreak havoc on our memory function. Inadequate sleep, poor nutrition, minimal physical activity, and high stress levels can significantly impair memory. Lack of proper rest inhibits the brain's ability to consolidate memories. Nutritional deficiencies hinder cognitive function, affecting memory processing. Physical inactivity reduces blood flow to the brain, limiting its ability to function optimally. Chronic stress results in hormonal imbalances that can damage memory-forming areas of the brain. Cumulatively, these habits create a detrimental environment for maintaining and forming effective memory processes.

So, what exactly constitutes a "bad habit"? It's more than just a routine; it's a behavior that hinders personal growth, productivity, and even memory over time. From the procrastination that delays progress to the mindless distractions that fracture our focus, these habits create a subtle undercurrent that influences how we navigate our lives. Bad habits act as silent saboteurs, impeding our ability to get things done efficiently and leaving a lingering residue on our cognitive functions.

Recognizing the gravity of negative habits is not merely an exercise in self-awareness; it is a vital step toward personal growth. This introspective journey is not about casting judgment but about unraveling the grip of these habits, understanding their influence, and cultivating a mindset that fosters positive change.

We'll discuss the psychology of habits, understanding the habit loop and the neurological pathways they carve in our brains. Then, we'll explore practical strategies, from identifying common obstacles to breaking bad habits to embracing the power of habit replacement and habit stacking. It's an invitation to peel back the layers, confront the subtle saboteurs, and pave the way for a more productive, focused, and memory-enhanced life.

The Psychology of Bad Habits

The Habit Loop

The habit loop—an ingrained sequence of cue, routine, and reward—is a fundamental framework governing human behavior. Each component plays a unique role in the formation and perpetuation of habits, shaping our daily lives. To comprehend how our habits are reinforced, it's essential to dive deeper into the mechanics of this loop.

- **Cue:** The cue is the initiating factor of the habit loop. It acts as a signal that prompts a behavioral response. These cues can be diverse, ranging from emotional states and environmental stimuli to specific times of day. By recognizing and understanding these triggers, we gain valuable insights into the root causes of our habits, laying the groundwork for effective habit management.

- **Routine:** The routine, which is the observable behavior that follows the cue, is the tangible manifestation of habit formation. Repetition of this routine strengthens the neural connections in the brain, solidifying the habit loop. Analyzing and comprehending these routines is pivotal, and it offers a nuanced understanding of the behavioral patterns that influence our daily lives.

- **Reward:** Rewards act as the driving force behind the habit loop, providing the brain with a sense of pleasure and satisfaction. This positive reinforcement, facilitated by the release of dopamine, creates a feedback loop that motivates repetition of the routine. Understanding the role of rewards is paramount; it elucidates why habits become deeply ingrained and resistant to change over time.

Neurological Basis of Habits

- **Neural Pathways:** Habitual behaviors leave a lasting imprint on the brain in the form of neural pathways. These pathways, akin to well-trodden mental routes, become more defined with each repetition. The brain's capacity to carve these pathways highlights its adaptability and proves that there is potential for rewiring and change in the face of habitual behaviors.

- **Plasticity and Change:** Neuroplasticity, the brain's ability to reorganize itself, is a key ally in the process of habit transformation. This phenomenon allows the brain to adapt new patterns of behavior, presenting an opportunity to break free from old habits and establish healthier ones. The brain's plasticity reinforces the notion that change is not only possible but inherent in our neurobiology.

The Impact of Habits on Memory

Habits and memory share and profound connection. The formation of habits influences cognitive processes that impact our ability to focus, learn, and remember information. By recognizing this cognitive link, we appreciate that our habits extend beyond mere actions; they shape our cognition and influence how we process and retain information.

Bad habits contribute to cognitive load, adding mental clutter that impairs optimal cognitive functioning. The cumulative effect of habitual behaviors can hinder our ability to concentrate, learn, and recall information efficiently.

Sound Familiar?

The habit loop is not an abstract concept confined to psychological theories; it is a dynamic force woven into our everyday lives. Consider those instances when tasks appear daunting, and the immediate response is to postpone them. Reflect on the reflexive reach for your smartphone when confronted with moments of idleness. These commonplace scenarios are not mere anecdotes; they are vivid snapshots of the habit loop unfolding in real-time, shaping the contours of our routines and behaviors.

When confronted with challenging tasks, the initiation of the habit loop begins with a cue—perhaps the feeling of discomfort or the perception of difficulty. This cue triggers the routine, often manifesting as procrastination, a habitual response that offers temporary relief from the perceived challenge. The habitual act of postponing tasks then leads to a reward, a momentary respite from the discomfort.

Likewise, the habitual pull toward a smartphone during moments of boredom follows a similar pattern. The cue here is the feeling of monotony, prompting the routine of reaching for the device, seeking the reward of instant entertainment or distraction. These seemingly small actions, when repeated over time, solidify the habit loop, creating well-trodden mental pathways.

What makes the habit loop profoundly relatable is its universality. It is not confined to specific individuals or isolated experiences. Everyone, at some point, has found themselves entangled in the loops of habit, whether it's the procrastination-induced delay of challenging tasks or the smartphone-scrolling reflex during moments of boredom.

Getting Rid of Negative Habits

Overcoming Common Obstacles

Breaking free from negative habits is often met with a set of common obstacles that can impede progress. One prevalent challenge is the allure of instant gratification—our inclination towards immediate rewards, even when they undermine our long-term goals. This short-term focus can make it difficult to resist the temptations that reinforce negative habits.

Another obstacle is the fear of discomfort associated with change. Humans, by nature, seek comfort and familiarity, and deviating from established routines can evoke anxiety. Overcoming this fear necessitates embracing the discomfort as a natural part of growth and recognizing that lasting change often requires stepping outside the comfort zone.

Moreover, the sheer magnitude of change can be overwhelming. Breaking a habit is a process that demands patience and resilience. The key lies in breaking down the journey into manageable steps, making the path forward more navigable.

Understanding and acknowledging these common obstacles is the initial stride toward overcoming them. By recognizing the allure of instant gratification, confronting the fear of discomfort, and breaking down change into manageable increments, individuals can lay the foundation for successful habit transformation. In the subsequent sections, we'll discuss strategies to address these obstacles and pave the way for lasting positive change.

The Power of Self-Awareness

In the pursuit of shedding negative habits, self-awareness emerges as a potent catalyst for change. It is the conscious acknowledgment and understanding of one's thoughts, emotions, and behaviors—a crucial first step toward breaking the shackles of detrimental habits.

Self-awareness brings to light the subtle cues and triggers that initiate the habit loop. By actively observing our responses and reactions, we gain insight into the patterns that fuel negative behaviors. This heightened awareness acts as a compass, guides us through the labyrinth of ingrained habits, and provides the clarity needed to recognize them in real time.

Moreover, self-awareness cultivates a sense of accountability. It empowers individuals to take ownership of their actions, fostering a mindset conducive to change. When armed with self-awareness, individuals can navigate challenges with a proactive mindset and make conscious choices that align with their overarching goals.

Mindful self-reflection, journaling, and regular check-ins are invaluable tools in nurturing self-awareness. If you examine your own thought processes, you can unlock the potential for transformative change. The power of self-awareness lies not just in understanding our habits but in our ability to redefine and redirect our responses toward a more positive and intentional future.

Making Room for Good Habits

Habits and Mental Space

Beyond shaping our physical routines, habits significantly impact our mental real estate. Like clutter in a room, bad habits divert attention and energy away from positive endeavors. Recognizing this dual impact prompts a conscious exploration of decluttering the mind—an exercise that is not only metaphorical but also a tangible process of creating room for transformative change.

The multifaceted influence of habits becomes apparent when we consider the mental space they occupy. It goes beyond the simple act of breaking free from physical routines; it entails untangling the threads woven into our thoughts. As we comprehend the depth of this mental occupancy, intentionally shedding detrimental habits becomes an act of liberation. This, in turn, nurtures an environment conducive to embracing positive changes.

Psychological and Emotional Benefits

The act of letting go of detrimental habits initiates a profound ripple effect, ushering in an array of psychological and emotional benefits. Liberation from the shackles of negative behaviors is more than a surface-level transformation; it is an emotional journey toward empowerment and self-discovery. The weight lifted is not just the burden of habits; it's the emotional baggage that accompanies them.

These psychological and emotional benefits extend beyond stress reduction and anxiety alleviation. They encompass a fundamental shift in how we perceive ourselves. Confidence and a positive self-image emerge as natural byproducts of this process. You'll not only break bad habits but also improve your sense of self-control and agency. The emotional liberation becomes a cornerstone for a renewed sense of identity and a strengthened mental resilience.

Benefits of Habitual Renewal

As detrimental habits gracefully fade away, the psychological and emotional renewal unfolds as a multifaceted phenomenon. The release of mental clutter doesn't merely enhance focus and concentration; it sets the stage for a comprehensive cognitive upgrade. The newfound mental clarity is not just a tool for efficiency but a gateway to embracing positive habits.

The benefits of habitual renewal extend into a holistic transformation—one that encompasses cognitive, emotional, and spiritual dimensions. It's not a mere swapping of negative for positive behaviors; it's a journey of self-evolution. The space created by breaking bad habits becomes a canvas for intentional living, where individuals can paint a vibrant picture of their desired future.

Building Positive Habits

Habit Replacement

Building positive habits is a transformative journey, and at its core lies a crucial strategy: habit replacement. This method is about intentionally substituting negative habits with positive alternatives. It's not just about eliminating the bad; it's a practical act of rewiring our habitual responses.

Habits are ingrained patterns in our brains, like well-worn paths. By intentionally replacing negative habits, we actively reprogram these neural pathways. It's a dynamic process that allows you to cultivate a positive and sustainable lifestyle.

Think of it as a deliberate and practical renovation project for your habits. Instead of leaving empty spaces, you fill them with intentional actions. This isn't just a change in routine; it's a fundamental reshaping of how you navigate daily life.

In essence, habit replacement is a hands-on approach to redefining behavior. It's not overly complex; it's about making intentional choices in the areas where negative habits once held sway. This practical rewiring paves the way for positive and lasting change.

The Importance of SMART Goals

In the process of developing habits, setting goals plays a crucial role in achieving positive changes. Consider this as the planning stage of your habit journey, where SMART goals—Specific, Measurable, Achievable, Relevant, and Time-bound—act as a guiding light.

- **Specificity:** Specificity becomes your trusted guide, offering a crystal-clear roadmap through the labyrinth of habit development. You should pinpoint exactly what you aim to achieve. This specificity transforms mere aspirations into tangible progress, ensuring that each step is deliberate and purposeful.

- **Measurability:** Measurability acts as the rhythm that transforms your goals into quantifiable milestones. As you embark on your habit journey, this measurable approach allows you to track progress and witness the tangible impact of your efforts. It's not limited to vague notions of improvement but concrete evidence of your journey towards positive change.

- **Achievability:** Achievability sets the tone for realism in your pursuits. Instead of reaching for the stars in a single bound, achievable goals recognize the value of steady progress. It's about setting milestones that stretch your capabilities but remain within the realm of attainability. This realistic approach favors a sense of accomplishment at each stage of your habit evolution.

- **Relevance:** Relevance takes center stage by aligning your goals with overarching objectives. It's not just about what you can do but what truly matters to you. Relevant goals resonate with your core values and aspirations, infusing your habit-building journey with a deeper sense of purpose.

- **Time-Bound:** Time-bound constraints act as the tempo, infusing a sense of urgency into your habit choreography. Setting deadlines creates a dynamic rhythm, propelling you forward with purpose and efficiency. It allows you to make a focused and timely progression towards your habit goals.

The Power of Consistency and Gradual Progression

When we explore positive habit-building, two powerhouse principles stand out: consistency and gradual progression. These aren't abstract concepts; they're the practical engines that turn sporadic efforts into sustainable habits.

Consistency is your steadfast companion, providing a reliable rhythm that transforms occasional actions into seamless routines. Don't limit yourself to occasional bursts of effort; focus on the steady beat that forges neural connections and embeds these habits into your daily life. Think of it as the reliable backbone that ensures that your positive habits become an integral part of who you are. By engaging in positive behaviors consistently, you're not just going through the motions; you're actively rewiring your brain. Each small, consistent action is like a building block, constructing a sturdy foundation for lasting habits.

Gradual progression complements consistency, recognizing that sustainable change doesn't happen overnight. It's not a sprint but a steady marathon. Starting with manageable actions and gradually increasing complexity isn't a lofty strategy; it's a practical approach that ensures the integration of positive habits is both sustainable and achievable. Picture it as a deliberate climb up a staircase, each step building upon the last. It's a methodical journey, avoiding the pitfalls of overwhelm that often accompany abrupt changes. This pragmatic approach doesn't just build habits; it cultivates resilience—a practical strength that helps you navigate life's challenges.

Habit Stacking for Memory Improvement

What Is Habit Stacking?

Habit stacking is a practical strategy that involves integrating new behaviors into existing routines, creating a seamless and efficient structure. In the context of memory improvement, habit stacking becomes a powerful tool for building a routine that not only supports but enhances cognitive functions.

Imagine it as the art of layering—adding new threads to your daily habits. Instead of viewing habits in isolation, habit stacking capitalizes on the efficiency of piggybacking new behaviors onto established ones. This intentional integration facilitates the process of memory enhancement by leveraging the existing infrastructure of your routine.

For example, while brushing your teeth each morning and/or evening—a deeply ingrained routine—try to recall three things you learned the previous day. This practice not only utilizes an existing habit but also encourages regular reflection and memory recall, effectively boosting cognitive functions without adding significant time or effort to your daily routine.

Tailoring to Individual Preferences

The beauty of habit stacking lies in its adaptability to individual preferences. It's not a one-size-fits-all approach; rather, it's a customizable framework that aligns with your existing habits and personal interests. If you're a book enthusiast, consider linking memory exercises to your reading routine. For those who enjoy cooking, use that time to mentally recall a list or practice memorizing new information related to food.

Tailoring habit stacking to individual preferences ensures that memory-enhancing activities seamlessly integrate into your lifestyle. It's a personalized approach that recognizes the uniqueness of each individual's routines and preferences.

Enhancing Retention and Recall through Association

The magic of habit stacking for memory improvement lies in the power of association. By linking memory-enhancing activities with established habits, you create mental connections that enhance retention and recall. The brain thrives on patterns, and habit stacking provides a structured way to reinforce positive cognitive behaviors.

As you consistently associate memory-improving activities with daily habits, you're essentially telling your brain, "This is important." The familiarity of the routine, coupled with the cognitive exercise, creates a synergistic effect that enhances memory functions. Over time, these associations become ingrained, contributing to improved retention and recall abilities.

For instance, if your morning routine involves brewing coffee, use that time to engage in a short memory exercise. It could be reviewing a list of important facts or recalling details from the previous day.

Similarly, if you have a daily walk, use this habitual activity to listen to educational podcasts or practice memorization exercises. By associating memory-enhancing tasks with established habits, you're not adding more to your plate; you're strategically integrating cognitive exercises into activities you already perform.

Conclusion

In this chapter, we've discussed the psychology of habits, dissected the habit loop, and explored the neurological underpinnings that intertwine with memory. The familiarity of detrimental habits echoes through our experiences, but the power to transform lies in our hands.

Dispelling negative habits requires a strategic approach, overcoming common obstacles, and harnessing the potent force of self-awareness. As we bid farewell to detrimental patterns, we make space for habits that nourish our mental well-being. The psychological and emotional benefits of positive habits make us recognize the profound impact on mental space and overall cognitive function. The concept of habitual renewal emerges as a beacon, emphasizing the ongoing process of cultivating positive behaviors.

Building positive habits involves deliberate steps, from habit replacement to setting SMART goals and embracing the power of consistency. The technique of habit stacking becomes a practical tool for memory improvement, allowing for enhanced retention and recall through strategic associations. In essence, this chapter serves as a blueprint for shedding old, counterproductive habits and forging a path toward cognitive vitality and continual self-improvement.

Chapter Seven

Use Your Tools and Resources

In our busy lives, productivity tools act like a guiding light amidst the chaos. These tools, both pragmatic and empowering, help us in our quest for improved memory and efficient time management. It's crucial to grasp the essence of productivity tools as not just accessories but as potent instruments that can redefine the way we approach our tasks.

Picture your productivity tools as an extension of your cognitive abilities, an external memory bank that supplements your mental prowess. In a world inundated with information, deadlines, and commitments, these tools become the organizational backbone that steadies your path. They are the architects of order in the cacophony of daily demands, allowing you to navigate seamlessly through the myriad tasks that make up your life.

These tools are diverse and range from the traditional to the cutting-edge. Notebooks, planners, and whiteboards stand as stalwarts of the analog realm, offering a tangible and tactile means of recording and organizing information. On the digital frontier, smartphones, tablets, and laptops emerge as dynamic companions, housing an array of apps and software designed to augment productivity.

The true magic of productivity tools lies in their ability to synthesize and simplify. They absorb the complexity of our schedules, commitments, and goals, distilling them into manageable units that we can readily comprehend. Imagine your tasks as pieces of a puzzle, scattered and perplexing until you deploy your productivity tools to assemble them into a coherent picture. They are more than mere crutches for a weak memory. They serve as strategic partners, amplifying your cognitive abilities and acting as force multipliers in your pursuit of excellence.

Calendar Mastery

Mastering your calendar is like following a map for navigating your daily life. A well-maintained calendar is way more than a chronicle of dates; it is a dynamic tool that orchestrates your time, aligning your efforts with the rhythm of your responsibilities. As we explore calendar mastery, think of it not just as a scheduling tool but as the conductor directing your daily activities.

At its core, a calendar is a visual representation of your commitments, deadlines, and priorities. It acts like a guardian, preventing forgetfulness and making sure no task is forgotten. To master your calendar, commit to turning this seemingly simple tool into a strategic asset for better memory and productivity.

Start by embracing the digital prowess of calendar apps. Platforms like Google Calendar, Microsoft Outlook, or Apple Calendar transcend the limitations of traditional paper planners. They offer dynamic features such as reminders, alerts, and synchronized access across multiple devices. Harnessing the power of these digital calendars allows you to move beyond the static nature of traditional calendars, infusing flexibility and responsiveness into your schedule.

Break down your tasks into manageable time blocks, assigning specific periods for focused work, breaks, and personal commitments. This deliberate structuring transforms your calendar into a roadmap, providing a clear trajectory for your day and mitigating the overwhelming sensation of an endless to-do list.

One of the pivotal aspects of calendar mastery is the cultivation of the habit of regular updates. Treat your calendar as a living document, evolving alongside your changing priorities and commitments. Consistent updates empower you to stay ahead of your schedule, anticipating deadlines and allowing for strategic planning that aligns with your overarching goals.

As we progress through this exploration, remember that calendar mastery is not about rigidly adhering to a schedule but about wielding your calendar as a strategic ally.

Task Management Systems

In the labyrinth of daily tasks, the concept of task management systems emerges as a guiding philosophy—a compass to navigate the complexities of responsibilities and priorities. Understanding and implementing an effective task management system is not just about creating to-do lists; it's a strategic approach to decluttering the mind, prioritizing objectives, and ensuring that each moment contributes to your goals.

At its core, a task management system is a methodology that empowers you to break down your workload into manageable components. The famed Getting Things Done (GTD) methodology pioneered by David Allen exemplifies this approach. GTD encourages the capture of all tasks in an external system, freeing the mind from the burden of remembering every detail and allowing it to focus on execution.

Begin by adopting a task management app or system that aligns with your workflow. Apps like Todoist, Trello, and Asana are designed to facilitate the implementation of task management methodologies seamlessly. These tools become the canvas upon which you paint the picture of your productivity journey, with each task serving as a stroke contributing to your accomplishments.

One of the fundamental principles of effective task management is the classification of tasks based on urgency and importance. The Eisenhower Matrix, a time-honored tool, categorizes tasks into four quadrants—urgent and important, important but not urgent, urgent but not important, and neither urgent nor important. This classification aids in prioritization, ensuring that your focus is directed towards tasks that truly matter.

Embrace the habit of regular reviews within your task management system. Schedule dedicated moments to assess and reassess your tasks, adjusting priorities as your goals evolve. The dynamism of your task management system lies in its responsiveness to change, enabling you to adapt to shifting priorities and unexpected demands with finesse.

Note-Taking Techniques

In the pursuit of memory enhancement and optimal productivity, the role of effective note-taking techniques cannot be overstated. Notes, when strategically captured and organized, become the building blocks of a fortified memory and a well-structured thought process. As we explore this crucial facet, envision your notes not merely as jottings on paper or digital screens but as a dynamic reservoir where insights, ideas, and important information converge for future use.

Consider note-taking as a deliberate act, a conscious effort to externalize the contents of your mind. Whether scribbled on a notepad or typed into a digital application, your notes serve as external memory banks, preserving the nuances of your thoughts and experiences. This intentional act of capturing information acts as a catalyst for memory retention and cognitive reinforcement.

Embrace the versatility of digital note-taking apps such as Evernote, Microsoft OneNote, or Notion. These apps transcend the limitations of traditional paper, offering features like searchability, multimedia integration, and cloud synchronization. Your notes become dynamic repositories, easily accessible and searchable whenever you need to revisit a concept, idea, or detail.

Develop a systematic approach to your note-taking tailored to your personal preferences and the nature of the information. Whether it's the Cornell Method, mind mapping, or the outline method, choose a technique that resonates with your learning style and the context of the material. The goal is not just to transcribe information but to distill it into a format that facilitates comprehension and recall.

As you cultivate the habit of note-taking, think beyond the classroom or workplace. Capture insights from books, podcasts, meetings, and personal reflections. Your notes should serve as a curated knowledge base, a place from which you can draw inspiration, ideas, and solutions to challenges. The act of revisiting and reinforcing these notes embeds the information into your long-term memory.

Using Smart Devices

The ubiquitous presence of smart devices transforms these pocket-sized marvels into indispensable tools for navigating the demands of daily life. Beyond their role as communication devices, smartphones, tablets, and smartwatches are equipped with features that can be harnessed strategically to elevate both productivity and memory.

Think of your smartphone as more than just a convenience. It's like a portable command center for your tasks and activities. Embrace its potential as more than a repository for apps and contacts; view it as an extension of your memory and an orchestrator of your tasks. The synergy between your smart device and productivity apps is crucial for achieving an efficient and organized lifestyle.

Leverage the power of voice assistants embedded in your smart devices. Whether it's Siri, Google Assistant, or Alexa, these virtual aides can transcribe your thoughts, set reminders, and initiate tasks with a simple vocal command. Embracing hands-free interactions minimizes disruptions, allowing a more fluid engagement with your surroundings while staying on top of your commitments.

Explore the capabilities of alarms and notifications to punctuate your day with gentle nudges. Set reminders for important meetings, deadlines, and even personal self-care routines. The strategic use of these prompts transforms your smart device into a proactive partner, ensuring that crucial tasks are not overshadowed in the whirlwind of daily activities.

Maximize the potential of your tablet for dynamic note-taking during meetings or brainstorming sessions. The larger screen real estate provides an expansive canvas for ideation, sketching diagrams, or collaboratively annotating documents. The fluidity of digital ink on tablet screens not only mirrors the tactile nature of traditional note-taking but also introduces a layer of interactivity and accessibility.

For those adorned with smartwatches, witness the convergence of style and functionality. Receive discreet notifications, monitor your daily activity, and even glance at your upcoming appointments—all from the convenience of your wrist. The unobtrusive nature of smartwatches ensures that pertinent information is at your fingertips without disrupting the rhythm of your day.

Memory Apps and Games

In the pursuit of sharpening memory and cognitive acuity, the digital realm offers a plethora of specialized apps and games designed to be both engaging and effective. These applications transcend the traditional notion of entertainment, evolving into strategic tools that stimulate and fortify the neural pathways responsible for memory. Envision these memory apps and games not as diversions but as targeted exercises for mental fitness.

Explore memory apps, where innovative tools are crafted to challenge and enhance your cognitive capabilities. Applications such as Lumosity, Elevate, and Peak offer a gamified approach to memory improvement, presenting a variety of exercises that encompass memory recall, pattern recognition, and logical reasoning. By integrating these apps into your routine, you transform moments of leisure into opportunities for cognitive development.

Engage with memory games that go beyond mere amusement to serve as purposeful workouts for your brain. Sudoku, crossword puzzles, and memory-matching games stimulate different facets of cognitive function, promoting mental agility and strategic thinking. Regular participation in these activities not only entertains but also contributes to the cultivation of a robust and resilient memory.

Consider incorporating language learning apps into your repertoire. Platforms like Duolingo, Babbel, or Memrise not only offer linguistic proficiency but also challenge your memory with vocabulary retention and pattern recognition. The dual benefit of acquiring a new skill while enhancing memory underscores the strategic value of these applications in your cognitive toolkit.

Embrace the scientific principles behind these memory apps and games. Neuroplasticity is stimulated through consistent mental exercises. By engaging in activities that challenge memory recall, spatial reasoning, and problem-solving, you foster an environment where your brain becomes more adept at processing and retaining information.

Customize Your Productivity Toolbox

The effectiveness of your toolkit lies in its alignment with your individual needs and preferences. An approach that fits everyone may not be the best fit for all, and customization becomes the key to transforming your toolbox into a personalized arsenal. Consider your toolkit not as a static set of prescribed tools but as a dynamic ensemble that evolves with your unique requirements.

Begin by assessing your personal workflow, identifying the tasks and challenges that are integral to your daily life. Consider your strengths, preferences, and the nature of your responsibilities. Your toolbox should be a reflection of your individuality—a tailored set of instruments that resonate with your cognitive style and facilitate your journey toward efficiency.

Explore the variety of productivity apps and tools available, but do so with a discerning eye. Experiment with different task management apps, calendars, and note-taking methods to identify what resonates with your workflow. Whether you find solace in a minimalist approach or thrive amidst a plethora of features, the goal is to curate a toolkit that seamlessly integrates with your habits and preferences.

Customization extends beyond digital tools to encompass the physical realm. If the tactile sensation of writing on paper sparks creativity and enhances memory for you, incorporate traditional tools like notebooks, journals, or whiteboards into your repertoire. The juxtaposition of analog and digital elements can create a balanced system that caters to different aspects of your cognitive process.

Consider the role of aesthetic appeal in your toolkit. A visually pleasing and well-organized environment can contribute to a positive mindset and increased focus. Explore themes, color-coding, and layouts that resonate with your sense of aesthetics. A visually curated workspace or digital interface can elevate your overall experience and make your toolkit more inviting.

Recognize that customization is an ongoing process. As your needs evolve and new tools emerge, be open to adjusting your toolkit accordingly. Regularly assess the effectiveness of each tool and make informed decisions about what enhances your productivity and contributes to an improved memory.

Balancing Digital and Analog

The difference between digital and analog offers various options to explore. The synergy between these two worlds, each with its unique strengths, fosters a balanced approach that caters to diverse cognitive preferences. You needn't choose between the pixelated and the tangible; use a strategic fusion that harmonizes the best of both worlds.

Commence by acknowledging the advantages of the digital domain. Smart devices, productivity apps, and digital note-taking offer efficiency, accessibility, and seamless integration into the fast-paced rhythm of modern life. Embrace the speed and convenience of digital tools, allowing them to be the swift facilitators of your tasks, reminders, and information retrieval.

Simultaneously, recognize the enduring value of analog tools. The tactile act of writing on paper engages different neural pathways, fostering a deeper connection with the information at hand. Consider incorporating physical notebooks, planners, and handwritten notes into your toolkit.

The deliberate pace of analog tools can provide moments of reflection and enhance the encoding of information into your memory.

Strive for a complementary relationship between the digital and analog facets of your toolkit. Use your digital calendar to set broad deadlines and reminders, and employ a physical planner for more detailed day-to-day scheduling. Merge the flexibility of digital note-taking with the sensory experience of jotting down ideas in a tangible notebook.

Explore the concept of "analog weekends" or dedicated periods where you deliberately disconnect from digital devices. This intentional break provides a mental reset and allows you to approach tasks with renewed focus and energy when re-engaging with the digital stuff.

As you navigate this blend, remain attuned to your personal preferences. Some may find solace in the streamlined efficiency of a fully digital system, while others may revel in the tactile pleasures of a predominantly analog approach. The key lies in finding the equilibrium that resonates with your cognitive style and enhances your overall sense of well-being.

Overcoming Common Challenges

The path toward memory enhancement and optimal productivity is not without its challenges. Recognizing and surmounting these obstacles is integral to the journey toward a more efficient and memorable life. Approach these challenges with a mindset of resilience and adaptability. Each obstacle encountered presents an opportunity for refinement and growth.

Procrastination

- Challenge: The allure of procrastination can be a formidable adversary, diverting attention from crucial tasks and eroding productivity.

- Solution: Break tasks into smaller, more manageable components. Set clear deadlines and employ techniques like the Pomodoro technique to structure focused work intervals with short breaks.

Information Overload

- Challenge: In a world inundated with information, the risk of cognitive overload is real, hindering memory retention and decision-making.

- Solution: Prioritize information, categorize tasks, and leverage your customized toolkit to filter out non-essential details. Regularly review and declutter your digital and physical spaces.

Tool Fatigue

- Challenge: Experimenting with a multitude of productivity tools can lead to tool fatigue, in which the abundance of options becomes overwhelming.

- Solution: Periodically assess the effectiveness of your tools and streamline your toolkit. Identify the core tools that align with your needs, discarding those that do not contribute significantly to your workflow.

Lack of Consistency

- Challenge: Inconsistency in the application of productivity methods can undermine their effectiveness.

- Solution: Establish consistent routines and habits. Set designated times for tasks like planning, reviewing your calendar, and updating your to-do list. Consistency helps with discipline and reinforces the integration of productivity tools into your daily life.

Failure to Prioritize

- Challenge: Without clear priorities, time and energy may be diverted to less impactful tasks, impeding progress on essential goals.

- Solution: Regularly reassess your priorities and align them with overarching objectives. Use task management systems to categorize tasks based on urgency and importance. Focus on high-priority tasks that contribute significantly to your long-term goals.

Lack of Self-Awareness

- Challenge: Rushing through tasks without self-awareness diminishes the quality of work and inhibits memory retention.

- Solution: Cultivate mindfulness in your daily activities. Approach tasks with intention and full attention. Engage in activities like meditation to enhance focus and reduce mental clutter.

Conclusion

Our exploration has equipped us with a comprehensive understanding of leveraging tools for optimal productivity and cognitive enhancement. We mastered the art of calendar management, recognizing its pivotal role in orchestrating our daily lives with precision.

Navigating the realm of task management systems, we uncovered efficient methods to organize and prioritize our responsibilities. Implementing note-taking techniques became a practical skill, enhancing our ability to capture and retain information effectively. The integration of smart devices, coupled with memory apps and games, provided us with a dynamic digital toolkit for cognitive support.

Customizing our toolbox emerged as a key theme, acknowledging the uniqueness of individual preferences and needs. Striking a balance between digital and analog tools allowed for a tailored approach, addressing the diverse ways we process information.

As we explored the chapter's challenges, from procrastination to information overload and tool fatigue, we uncovered strategies to overcome these common hurdles. Addressing the lack of consistency, failure to prioritize, and fostering self-awareness became integral components of our journey toward optimal tool utilization.

In essence, this chapter serves as a guide for navigating the vast array of tools and resources available, emphasizing their potential to enhance cognitive capabilities. By embracing customization, finding equilibrium between digital and analog, and tackling challenges head-on, we empower ourselves to harness these tools effectively, transforming them from mere instruments into catalysts for sustained productivity and cognitive excellence.

Chapter Eight

Get Your Sh** Together

In this final chapter, we hone in on a no-frills, straight-talk discussion about something crucial: your mental health. We're delving into the practical side of things—how taking care of your mind is not just essential but downright foundational for beefing up your memory. We'll cut through the fluff, tackle challenges head-on, and lay out some practical strategies. This chapter is all about rolling up your sleeves, getting real, and ensuring your mental game is on point. After all, when it comes to sorting out your cognitive functions, it all starts with giving your mental health the attention it deserves.

Acknowledging Challenges

Embarking on the journey to enhance memory demands a candid recognition of the ubiquitous challenges that intersect with our efforts. These challenges, far from being idiosyncratic, form an integral part of the intricate process of cognitive refinement. To fortify our pursuit, a meticulous understanding of these challenges is indispensable, laying the foundation for targeted and effective solutions.

Life's manifold demands, characterized by ceaseless stress, persistent distractions, and the unyielding cadence of contemporary existence, erect formidable barriers on the path to memory improvement. In navigating this terrain, discernment is key. Identifying and comprehending these challenges enables a deliberate and informed approach to surmounting them. By confronting the realities of our circumstances, we empower ourselves to proactively address the impediments to memory enhancement.

Setbacks, an inescapable facet of any educational venture, are intrinsic to memory improvement. This acknowledgment is not an admission of inadequacy but a pragmatic acceptance of the iterative nature of learning. Viewing challenges as catalysts for growth transforms the narrative; setbacks become opportunities for refinement rather than insurmountable obstacles.

Understanding the specific challenges that punctuate our memory improvement journey is paramount. It is an acknowledgment that the demands of daily life, be they professional commitments or personal responsibilities, can exert considerable influence. By isolating these factors, we gain clarity, enabling a more nuanced and targeted approach to memory enhancement.

It is essential to underscore that acknowledging challenges is not an endpoint but a prelude to actionable solutions. The subsequent sections of this discourse are poised to unravel strategies and insights that align with the realities of our cognitive needs.

In conclusion, the act of acknowledging challenges is not merely a formality but a deliberate step toward empowerment. It is a testament to our resolve to confront these challenges head-on. You always have to keep in mind that memory improvement is not a linear trajectory; it is a dynamic process enriched by the acknowledgment of challenges and the unwavering commitment to surmounting them.

Importance of Mental Health

In the pursuit of memory enhancement, the pivotal role played by mental health emerges as a cornerstone, anchoring the entire edifice of cognitive refinement. The premise is clear: a robust cognitive architecture, synonymous with a healthy mind, forms the bedrock upon which optimal cognitive functions, notably memory retention and recall, are meticulously built. It is in recognizing this symbiotic relationship between mental health and cognitive prowess that we glean valuable insights into the foundational aspects of memory improvement.

The complex relationship between mental health and memory lapses is crucial. Chronic stress, an omnipresent companion in the contemporary landscape, unveils its disruptive potential on cognitive abilities. Its insidious influence extends beyond emotional strain, impacting concentration and introducing perturbations in the orchestration of memory processes. Recognizing stress is a significant factor that needs addressing to improve cognitive well-being.

You must aim for a comprehensive outlook because this holistic approach to mental health encompasses not only the absence of distress but the active cultivation of emotional well-being, adept stress management, and fortified psychological resilience. It becomes evident that a balanced mental state is not a passive outcome but an actively nurtured state, radiating positive effects on memory and the broader spectrum of cognitive capacities.

In practical terms, the implications of sustaining good mental health for memory enhancement unfold with practical significance. A stable mental state is akin to a fertile ground wherein the seeds of information not only find ready absorption but also take root for robust recall. The conscious commitment to mental well-being is a strategic investment in cognitive prowess, transforming it into a dynamic and responsive arena for effective learning, retention, and retrieval of information.

We also have to contemplate the enduring advantages of prioritizing mental health. Beyond the immediate gains in memory improvement, a sustained focus on mental well-being reveals its contributory role in fostering overall cognitive longevity. This dimension underscores the profound impact of mental health practices, positioning them as instrumental components in the trajectory of a proactive and enduring approach to cognitive enhancement.

Empowerment signifies recognizing the agency individuals possess in actively caring for their mental health. This recognition transcends mere acknowledgment, morphing into a call for intentional and strategic self-improvement. Mental health practices, viewed through the lens of personal empowerment, become not only tools for enhanced memory but also instruments for sculpting a resilient and enduring cognitive foundation.

The Power of Meditation

In the realm of cognitive refinement, meditation emerges as a formidable force, wielding transformative effects on various mental faculties including memory. At its core, meditation operates as a pragmatic tool, cultivating heightened awareness and mental acuity. This deliberate practice goes beyond a mere exercise in mindfulness, extending its influence to the intricate landscape of memory enhancement.

An inherent aspect of meditation is its pronounced role in stress reduction, and by extension, its consequential benefits for memory improvement. The calming effects induced by meditative practices serve as a counterbalance to stress—an acknowledged disruptor of cognitive functions, particularly memory. By mitigating the detrimental impacts of stress, meditation creates an environment conducive to efficient information recall and retention.

Regarding the neurological aspect, meditation exhibits a tangible impact on the brain, especially in areas intricately linked to memory and cognitive functions. Scientific insights underscore its potential to influence neural plasticity and fortify structures associated with memory. This empirical foundation solidifies meditation as a practical strategy for those seeking to enhance their memory capabilities through nuanced engagement with brain physiology.

In practical terms, the application of meditation techniques tailored for memory enhancement is becoming more evident. By incorporating specific meditation practices into daily routines, individuals can unlock benefits such as heightened concentration, improved information retention, and an overall amplification of memory capabilities. The utility of meditation lies not merely in its theoretical prowess but in its tangible integration into everyday life.

Consistency is crucial in the context of meditation for memory enhancement. The cumulative nature of its effects necessitates regular engagement to reap long-term benefits. A gradual and sustained approach is the hallmark of memory improvement through meditation, dispelling the notion of quick fixes in favor of a deliberate and enduring process.

Gradually weaving meditation into one's lifestyle stands as a pragmatic endeavor. Offering practical guidance, this section delineates actionable steps for individuals to incorporate meditation into their daily routines. By demystifying the integration process, it becomes an accessible and feasible strategy, positioning meditation as a practical and potent tool for those committed to their mental health.

In conclusion, the power of meditation lies not in esoteric notions but in its tangible impact on mental well-being and cognitive functions, particularly memory. It operates as a deliberate and systematic approach, leveraging its influence on stress reduction, neurological pathways, and practical applications to carve a path toward enhanced memory capabilities.

Unplugging and Relaxation Techniques

In our agitated modern life, it becomes imperative to cast a discerning eye upon stressors that extend beyond the confines of digital engagements. Beyond the palpable hum of technology, daily pressures, the weight of personal responsibilities, and the unrelenting expectations set by society collectively weave a complex tapestry of stress. Addressing these various stressors necessitates not merely acknowledgment but a proactive and deliberate approach, a conscious effort to safeguard and fortify our overall mental well-being.

Taking breaks becomes a universal imperative, irrespective of the specific sources of stress. Far from mere respites, these interludes stand as vital waypoints safeguarding against the looming specter of burnout. Beyond preservation, they become sanctuaries for cognitive vitality, offering precious moments of reprieve. The inherent value of these breaks lies not merely in the pause they provide but in their capacity to reintroduce a sense of balance, renew our energy, and instill a renewed focus in the face of incessant demands.

Practical relaxation techniques—versatile tools accessible to all—are central to this holistic approach. From the rhythmic cadence of deep breathing exercises to the joy of a warm bath or even the simplicity of listening to music, these techniques transcend the realm of standalone practices. They metamorphose into invaluable instruments for inducing relaxation and alleviating stress in its myriad forms. More than momentary reprieves, these techniques become steadfast companions, promoting a state of mental relaxation that resonates across various cognitive functions, subtly influencing memory, focus, and overall mental acuity.

The overarching ambition, then, is not just to sporadically deploy these relaxation practices but to seamlessly weave them into our daily existence. Flexibility is your ally as you try to personalize these moments of intentional relaxation. Whether embedded within the confines of demanding work hours, nestled within the comforting embrace of personal spaces, or skillfully interspersed amid daily responsibilities, these moments take on a bespoke quality. They cease to be extraneous pauses; they metamorphose into integral components of a sustainable and personalized routine. Here are eight examples of valuable relaxation techniques.

Deep-Breathing Exercises

Incorporating deep breathing into your routine is a fundamental yet potent tool for stress reduction. As you inhale deeply through your nose, feel your diaphragm expanding. As you exhale slowly through pursed lips, you activate the body's relaxation response. This simple technique not only calms the nervous system but also promotes a tangible sense of calm. Make it a habit, especially during hectic moments, to anchor yourself in the present with a few intentional breaths. It is a straightforward practice that has a remarkable impact on easing tension and cultivating a more composed state of mind.

Progressive Muscle Relaxation (PMR)

Progressive Muscle Relaxation (PMR) is a systematic approach to physical relaxation that holds profound benefits for overall well-being. By intentionally tensing and then gradually releasing each muscle group, starting from your toes and progressing to your head, you allow accumulated physical tension to dissipate. This practical technique is particularly effective in releasing the grip of stress on your body. As you integrate PMR into your routine, perhaps before bedtime or during breaks, you'll notice a tangible difference in how your body responds to stressors, paving the way for a more relaxed and composed you.

Aromatherapy

Harness the power of scent through aromatherapy to create an oasis of calm in your daily life. Inhale the soothing aroma of essential oils such as lavender, chamomile, or eucalyptus to induce a profound sense of relaxation. Whether through diffusers, inhalers, or diluted oils, the olfactory experience triggers a direct response in the brain, influencing mood and reducing stress. This uncomplicated yet effective practice is a practical addition to your self-care toolkit, easily adaptable to various settings. Experiment with different scents to discover which ones resonate with you, and let the subtle power of aromatherapy become a consistent and rejuvenating element in your daily routine.

Guided Imagery

Unlock the potential of your imagination through guided imagery, a practical tool for redirecting your focus and alleviating stress. Picture yourself in a tranquil environment; engage all your senses in the mental visualization. This deliberate mental escape from the demands of daily life creates a sanctuary within your mind. As you integrate guided imagery into moments of tension or as part of a dedicated practice, you'll find that this straightforward technique offers a respite for your mind, fostering a sense of calm and mental rejuvenation.

Warm Bath or Shower

Transform your daily routine into a therapeutic experience by incorporating warm baths or showers. Allow the soothing sensation of warm water to envelop your body, promoting physical and mental relaxation. This practical self-care ritual not only cleanses your body but also serves as a sanctuary for unwinding. Especially during moments of heightened stress, take the time to immerse yourself in the warmth. Let it melt away tension and leave you refreshed and revitalized. Embrace this simple yet powerful practice, turning the mundane act of bathing into a deliberate act of self-nurturing.

Listening to Music

Harness the therapeutic power of music as a practical tool for relaxation. Choose calming melodies that resonate with you, and immerse yourself in the auditory experience. Music has a direct impact on emotions, making it an accessible and effective way to shift your mood. Whether during work breaks, daily commutes, or intentional relaxation sessions, let the harmonies guide you into a state of tranquility. Consider creating personalized playlists tailored to your preferences, allowing music to become an ever-present ally in your journey toward a more relaxed and composed state of mind.

Autogenic Training

Discover the transformative effects of autogenic training, a practical technique centered around self-suggestions to induce deep relaxation. By focusing on sensations of warmth and heaviness in different parts of your body, you guide yourself into a state of profound calm. This intentional practice serves as a powerful ally in reducing stress and anxiety. Incorporate autogenic training into your routine, perhaps during moments of quiet reflection or as part of a bedtime ritual.

Yoga Nidra

Yoga nidra, or "yogic sleep," is a great relaxation technique. The core focus? Kicking stress to the curb. It is like a mental massage, systematically guiding you through your body to release tension and plunge you into a state of deep chill. It's not rocket science; it's about as uncomplicated as relaxation can get.

No need for a Ph.D. in meditation. Yoga nidra comes with a user-friendly script that leads you through simple steps. Breathe here, feel that, acknowledge those emotions—easy, right? It's meditation without the unnecessary complexity. Accessibility is the name of the game. Whether you're a meditation guru or a newbie, Yoga nidra welcomes all. No fancy gear required; just find a quiet spot, get comfy, and let the guided session do its thing.

It's not just about feeling Zen. Yoga nidra has been linked to better sleep. You snooze better, you consolidate memories better. That's as practical as it gets. No need to block off hours; a fifteen-minute session fits into your coffee break. It's a practical plug-and-play solution for whenever life cranks up the stress.

Want it tailor-made? Yoga nidra has you covered. Pick a session that suits your mood—relaxation, stress relief, or maybe even one to rev up your creativity. Personalized relaxation—now that's practical.

Non-Duality: The Ultimate Grail

If you want to get your life in order, the concept of non-duality offers a unique philosophical lens. Non-duality asserts a fundamental interconnectedness between the mind and body, challenging the notion of separateness.

The conventional dichotomies of success and failure are questioned by the principle of non-duality. Instead of viewing these as mutually exclusive, non-duality suggests an intertwined relationship between achievements and setbacks. Getting your sh** together requires transcending these dualistic perspectives, acknowledging that both success and failure contribute to personal growth in a unified manner.

Embracing imperfection becomes a key facet influenced by non-duality. Instead of judging moments as good or bad, the philosophy encourages acceptance of the present without attachment to labels. This approach enables a more flexible navigation of life's complexities, unburdened by rigid standards of success or failure.

Non-duality suggests that ego, often responsible for a false sense of separation, needs to be recognized and dissolved. You can navigate life with clarity attained through dissolving the ego. This process allows for a more authentic and integrated approach, aligning actions with a profound understanding of interconnectedness rather than being driven by a fragmented sense of self.

In this philosophical framework, the traditional boundaries of self and other, subject and object, dissolve, giving way to an understanding that transcends dualistic distinctions. Non-duality encourages a shift from divisive thinking to a holistic perspective, where acceptance becomes a guiding principle. It invites us to accept the totality of our experiences without judgment, recognizing that light and shadow and joy and sorrow are integral facets of the same intricate tapestry of life. Through acceptance grounded in non-duality, we release the shackles of polarized thinking and cultivate a more compassionate and inclusive approach to ourselves and the world. It is a transformative journey that invites us to surrender the illusion of separateness, fostering a profound acceptance of the inherent interconnectedness that defines the human experience.

Conclusion

Our journey through this chapter has been one of profound self-discovery and practical strategies for cultivating mental resilience. We commenced by acknowledging the challenges that life throws our way, recognizing that growth often emerges from navigating difficulties. The importance of mental health took center stage, emphasizing that a sound mind forms the foundation for effective memory and cognitive well-being.

We discussed the power of meditation and explored various techniques from deep breathing exercises to progressive muscle relaxation (PMR) and autogenic training. These methods, grounded in simplicity, offer tangible tools to manage stress and foster a sense of calm. The chapter unfolded with an exploration of other powerful strategies, each serving as a practical remedy for the demands of modern life. From aromatherapy to guided imagery, warm baths, and music, we found that these approaches not only alleviate stress but also contribute to a resilient mental landscape.

The concept of non-duality emerged as the ultimate grail, encouraging you to transcend dualistic thinking and embrace the interconnected nature of existence. This perspective invites us to release the illusion of separateness and recognize the oneness that underlies our experiences.

In essence, this is a call to action, urging us to prioritize mental well-being through practical, accessible tools. By acknowledging challenges, embracing relaxation techniques, and delving into the profound wisdom of non-duality, we pave the way for a resilient mind capable of navigating life's complexities with grace. This chapter serves as a roadmap for integrating these practices into our daily lives, fostering a holistic approach to mental health and setting the stage for an enriched and purposeful existence.

Conclusion

In concluding our journey through this book, I want to extend a heartfelt acknowledgment to each reader who has accompanied us on this transformative exploration. Your commitment to getting sh** done and enhancing your memory is commendable, and as we bid farewell to these pages, I want to leave you not just with a sense of accomplishment but with a profound motivation to continue this journey.

Improving memory is not a one-time feat; it's a dynamic and ongoing process that requires consistent effort and dedication. Consider this book as a stepping stone, a catalyst that has ignited your pursuit of cognitive excellence. Remember, just as muscles need regular exercise to stay strong, your mind benefits from continuous engagement and nurturing.

As you embark on the path ahead, let these words be a compass guiding you through the terrain of self-improvement. Embrace the challenges as opportunities for growth, acknowledging that setbacks are merely detours, not roadblocks. Think of the practical tools and techniques shared in this book as instruments in your personal orchestra, each playing a crucial role in the symphony of your mental well-being.

Here is a roadmap to carry forward.

- **Set Realistic Goals:** Define achievable milestones for your memory improvement journey. Break down the process into manageable steps, celebrating victories along the way.

- **Create Consistent Habits:** Make the techniques outlined in this book a part of your daily routine. Whether it's meditation, exercise, or dietary changes, consistency is the key to lasting change.

- **Stay Curious and Learn:** Cultivate a curious mindset. Challenge yourself to learn new things, explore diverse subjects, and keep your mind engaged. The more you feed your intellectual curiosity, the more robust your memory becomes.

- **Reflect and Adjust:** Periodically reflect on your progress. What's working well? What can be refined? Be open to adjustments, recognizing that the journey is as much about self-discovery as it is about memory enhancement.

- **Connect with Others:** Share your journey with like-minded individuals. Join communities, attend workshops, or engage in discussions about memory improvement. Learning from others and sharing your experiences can be profoundly motivating.

Remember, the pursuit is not a destination; it's a continuous process of self-discovery and improvement. With each intentional step forward, you are sculpting a sharper, more resilient memory and a more focused, purposeful mind. Embrace the ongoing nature of this journey, and let the passion for self-improvement be your guiding light. The pages of your memory await the stories you choose to write. Keep going, keep growing, and may your journey be as inspiring as the destination you envision.

About the Author

Deborah LeBlanc is a Certified Clinical Hypnotherapist with certifications in ten other healing modalities that span over seventy presenting issues. Her expertise in relationship-building has afforded her the opportunity to travel throughout the country as a keynote speaker and workshop facilitator.

www.ingramcontent.com/pod-product-compliance
Lightning Source LLC
Chambersburg PA
CBHW070111080526
44586CB00013B/1263